Léopold Sédar Senghor

William Kluback

Léopold Sédar Senghor

From Politics to Poetry

PETER LANG
New York • Washington, D.C./Baltimore
Bern • Frankfurt am Main • Berlin • Vienna • Paris

Library of Congress Cataloging-in-Publication Data

Kluback, William.
Léopold Sédar Senghor: from politics to poetry / William Kluback.
p. cm.
Includes bibliographical references.
1. Senghor, Léopold Sédar, 1906– —Criticism and interpretation. I. Title.
PQ3989.S47Z737 841—dc21 96-45380
ISBN 0-8204-3488-4

Die Deutsche Bibliothek-CIP-Einheitsaufnahme

Kluback, William:
Léopold Sédar Senghor: from politics to poetry / William Kluback.
–New York; Washington, D.C./ Baltimore; Bern; Frankfurt am Main;
Berlin; Vienna; Paris: Lang.
ISBN 0-8204-3488-4

Cover design by Wendy Lee.

This book is dedicated to the civilizations of the universal.

CONTENTS

Preface

This is a book of imagined conversations inspired by the work of the great twentieth-century African poet and statesman Léopold Sédar Senghor. We all know conversation as part of our daily life, and rely on its give-and-take to bind us to our family and friends, and to our local communities. It is the most human and humanizing of activities. We also enjoy the conversations of others that have been pursued in written form, as in letters between two thoughtful and articulate people. An exchange of letters, such as those between Leonard Woolf and his friends or between Harry Truman and his wife, however different the writers, offers a revealing view of relationships among people, of individual reflection and change over time, and thus an unequaled view of the human personality. Yet a third possibility for personal exchange is illustrated by this book. It presents us with the kind of conversation that can take place in the study when, at peace and at leisure, a curious and careful reader puts questions to the writers and philosophers of the past, searching their work for answers to problems that preoccupy him. Rarely are such conversations overheard, but Professor William Kluback, a philosopher who has written on connections between philosophy, religion, and poetry, has decided to put his conversations in print.

The man whose writings provided the occasion for these conversations, Léopold Sédar Senghor, believed in dialogue above all. Born poor in a small West African town in 1906, Senghor studied hard, first in French Catholic mission schools and later in secondary school and university in Paris. He became a prize-wining poet, an advisor to colonial ministers, and a deputy in the French National Assembly in the era when France thought of its colonies as extensions of itself. After the Algerian war, Senghor worked with de Gaulle to find a way for his native Senegal to become independent in friendship with France, and he then served as Senegal's first president from 1960-80. To crown his distinguished career, the Académie française voted Senghor its first

African member, thereby acknowledging him as one of the "immortals" whose work would endure beyond his lifetime.

As a poet and philosopher, Senghor has made an important contribution to the ongoing discussion about the meaning of life in our century. He offers to Europeans a wisdom distilled by a totally different culture. Unlike many voices from beyond the borders of Europe and America that clamor for a hearing, Senghor has listened to the voices of others. He has listened to the elders of his native land, to the classical philosophers of Greece, to the Christian prophesy, and to the voices of European philosophers, anthropologists, and poets. He prepared himself by diligent study before trying to catch the world's attention. When he had found his own distinctive point of view, he decided to describe and analyze the culture and values of black Africa, arguing that Africans have cultivated some aspects of human experience that have been neglected by Europeans. He supposed that each culture, African and European, could benefit from the wisdom of the other. Africans could contribute the values and experience of their culture, what Senghor called Negritude, to the developing universal civilization which would allow all of humankind to develop its true potential. What came to distinguish Senghor's work was his belief in the mutual benefit of dialogue, the back-and-forth of self and other, French and African, the subjective and the objective world. The existence of a multicultural world provides, Senghor points out, great opportunities for learning, if only each person can remain open to hearing what others have to say. Each culture has something of value to offer the others. Exclusion and the search for purity, racial or cultural, will lead, he writes, to diminution and even to death.

His has not been a facile stance. Senghor did not forget that French colonial policies enslaved his people, but he forces himself to remember that the French have also brought good to Africa – learning and the Christian God. His poetry reflects the effort and conflicting emotions spent on reconciling these facts, and his devotion to his French and African cultures. His poems written in Paris provide a glimpse of a lonely student far from home, sitting up late at night in a cheap student apartment, diligently studying and reflecting upon the philosophers and religious thinkers of an alien culture. In them and from them he finds confirmation of intuitions hitherto barely understood, new ways to consider the past and the relations among cultures, and above all, a personal language in which to contribute a new voice to Europeans' discussion of themselves and the world. Strengthened by a profound religious belief that assured him that reconciliation and harmony were always possible, he pursued an often difficult and discouraging search for a means to embrace both his French and African worlds.

Taking his lead from Senghor, William Kluback has asked his own questions of the twentieth-century philosophers Senghor most admired. He considers Jacques Maritain, Pierre Teilhard de Chardin, Paul Claudel, and Gaston Bachelard in the context of what the African, Senghor, sought and found in them. To their voices he adds that of Senghor, as a rare link between two traditions of thinking about the spiritual dimension of human experience. Like Senghor, Professor Kluback has not hesitated to ask the basic questions of ethics and philosophy about the relationship of God to man and the value of the individual personality. As he does, he also insists on the kinship of poetry and philosophy, and the connection of both to confident and effective action in the world. The result is a highly personal book that amplifies the contribution of an African voice to ongoing conversations about the value and significance of human life. While those who expect definitive answers will, as they always must, be disappointed, those who enjoy the quest will find good company here.

Janet G. Vaillant
Harvard University

1

The Conversation

I often wonder if it is possible to find a closing point for a spiritual conversation which has lasted for many years and has no visible end. I wonder whether the great conversations in which the writer engages with others is not really a single conversation which the spirit develops throughout its earthly adventures. Even when the speaking and listening grow silent, the voices are still there waiting to speak again. There are not many with whom we actually converse. With the many we have short and momentary talks. With the few there is continuity even in silence. The voice hovers over us like the shadows which never leave us. With Senghor, the shadows are always there reminding us of thoughts I never want to forget, but seem at times to be vague and distant. In all these conversations not only is someone talking to me, but I am talking to myself. I am discovering within me what is meaningful and vital to my life, what I am saying to others is really what others have been saying to me. But there is one difference: I have selected the voices I want to hear, the ideas that are working and creating within me. In other words, listening is a preparation for speaking. What I am prepared to hear determines what I am capable of saying. Often I ask myself why I say and believe what I utter, and I find that it is the past that comes back to me, at times distinctly, at others indistinctly. A friend, a poet, a philosopher, or a writer suddenly appears to me. I find the words of our conversation. They have never left me. They remain a part of my past. I cannot erase a past that is vastly different from an intellectual figment which others have constructed for me. In the depths of my words lives the self. It is this self that continuously speaks to me and to my friends. It is this self which speaks to Senghor.

In a book of conversations, *La Poésie de l'action*, Senghor was asked about the solitude which comes to writers and heads of state. He replied: "Surely I feel solitude because I have not yet seen the realization of my utopia, of my folly."[1] Here lies that consequence which many men bear for their power. Solitude is both a happy and painful experience. It takes us from the thoughts and feelings of our fellowmen; it draws us toward a realm of ideas which we share with few. Our conversations become more and more selective and rare. We find less patience for the common pleasures of life and more for the world of creativity. Senghor notes that for him the significant word is *poiesis,* a word that goes far beyond poetry and speaks of making or creating. This word brings us close to divinity, a closeness which can be approached by no other reality. Senghor, through all his political and poetical dreams and reveries, would be that creator of the word and deed which gives us cause to wonder. We speak to him constantly because with him we find what each of us seeks in another being, that rare openness to beauty and human creativity. With him we speak of the real and the ideal and we ask if there is truly a difference between them beyond the creation of the artist. We need the ideal to give us the future. We need the real to tell us how difficult is the journey to the promised land. We always need to talk to find out what is happening within us, what happens when we speak to Senghor, and why it happens in this or that particular way.

The more we read of Senghor, the more forceful becomes our conversation with him. I am awakened to feelings and ideas which I can discuss particularly with him. I am fascinated by the dialogues of cultures which embrace distant lands and peoples. Although I know that I am a man of a particular culture, living from biblical traditions and values, I want to know how other men live their relationships to God and their fellowmen, what art, sculpture, and architecture they have developed. If I can do no more than observe with admiration and comprehension, I have begun the intellectual and emotional voyage that constitutes spiritual life. Senghor remarked: "Whether I write a poem or decide upon a legal project, I am concerned with the same thing from different aspects. We are dealing with the transformation of the world, with the giving of life. My poem creates a new world for my readers, one in which they participate. I give them spiritual nourishment. It is the same when I promulgate a law."[2]

This use of the personal pronoun *I* is deeply significant. The speaking *I* does not simply express an individual experience. Its importance lies in the collective reality that is embodied in it. The *I* calls forth our persistent attempt to unify the experience we have lived, our attempt to give it meaning and purpose. We listen to this *I* speak. We

---

[1]*La Poésie de l'action* (Paris: Edition Stock, 1980), 233; unless otherwise noted, all translations are my own.
[2]Ibid., 235.

hear in it a world of relationship, of trials and battles, of successes and failures. In these we are always discovering our lives. We do this not to find identification, but to seek contrasts and similarities, and above all, to comprehend the creative process that each great man struggles to elaborate. We read notebooks, letters, memoirs, essays to find that intellectual movement from which the works of art and literature emerge. Senghor notes: "When I say 'I' there is in this personal pronoun more than myself. There is this people from whom I was born and in whose name I speak. But it is I who am this voice as Poet and President, who writes and speaks, who in speaking or writing, *creates a new world.* From the time of our independence I wanted to create or bring about a new philosophy, a new literature, art, economy, that is, a new society, a new *Senegalise Man*.... This is *poiesis,* and for this reason this book bears the title *The Poetry of Action.*"[3]

The *I* which many of us dare not utter and feel obliged to hide in heaps of abstract and mounting notes and details is one of the most precious words we have within us. The *I* reveals the experience we are capable of having with the self, the capacity to turn toward the self and explore the possibilities that lie within it. The *I* accompanies thinking, loving, imagining, the experiences that are vital and sacred to us. To Moses, God spoke those words that have continuously given us perplexity and an uncomfortable insecurity. He proclaimed: "I am who I am," and with these words God reminded us also of his words: "I will be who I will be." Our *I* finds no such identity; it creates its other or becomes an other to itself. It is the *I* of the human experience, of the creative experience. In this *I* we find the self as it comes forth in a poem, a book, an action. With Senghor, we learn the conversation of creativity. We sit with him as Socrates sat with his companions and we learn to speak with each other. Here lies the essence of learning, of the human relationship, discovering how to converse with each other, practicing the art of listening and imagining. We can all read Senghor, but we cannot all converse with him. Conversation takes time and needs practice. We must read and listen to the words we absorb. Reading becomes the art of reading. Listening becomes a distinct art.

Conversation is more than the exchanging of words. It is the source of creativity. In conversation with the other I clarify my ideas and comprehend my feelings. What the other says awakens in me new possibilities which I could not awaken in myself. I need the honesty and trust of the other. Senghor remarked that there were two words he detested: cowardice and disloyalty. The words interrupt the course of life; they cause us to doubt its purpose and the value of its order. Our

---

[3]Ibid., 235-36.

conversations take place within a life which must be meaningful and give us happiness. "Now I think," said Senghor, "that to live is to be happy, in other words, to create. Insofar as I created a new Senegal, I am happy. Insofar as I continue to write poems, I am happy. My greatest happiness is to take my poems after the first draft, and make of them pleasing words, both for the heart and the ear."[4] Happiness lies in creativity, in the making of a poem. We wonder about the process of its formation: How does the poem come to be? What is known and, unknown seem so interwoven that we surrender all possibility of drawing them apart. They belong to each other in such a way that we feel that the known and unknown will always be related through mystery and marvel. Happiness is the interplay of forces we control and those we don't. They dance and sing together and we are delighted to watch them through the *I* which gives voice to what is happening within and outside of us. Creativity excites us. We are enchanted by the images which come forth from our powers to make things. We honor the word *poiesis*.

We are constantly asked to think about the future. Thinking in this sense is to form an image, to articulate hopes, and to cultivate the right to dream. We look to Senghor and ask him to think about the future. He believed that one day "politics will be in the service of culture and not the reverse. "I see," he said, "a world where man having satisfied his 'animal needs' will be free to give himself to his 'generic activity,' that is, to create a new world by producing 'works of beauty.' I mean cultural goods as numerous as material ones."[5] We know how easily formed are these dreams of the future, and we turn away in skepticism, and often with disdain. The realities of life are too painful and chaotic to allow us to believe that man will change his wayward attitudes and become a loving creature. The reality that confronts us is always fleeting and we are equally skeptical about the permanence of laws and self-proclaimed necessities.

There is power in faith because it belongs to our experience. We fight for its reality in defiance of what is about us. Faith allows us to create a new world over and against the one that appears and claims to be real. With Senghor, we can speak often about the human power to set aside the destiny of life and to create another description of man's relationships to nature and society. We read the biblical prophets and psalms and we wonder at their images, pain accompanied by hope, degradation yielding to optimism. We realize that there is a balance which must be found between the visions which arise from human evil

[4]Ibid., 236-37.
[5]Ibid., 348.

and those that emerge from love and trust in God. Senghor knows these problems. We find him ready to speak to those who listen and want to converse with him.

Beyond all the reflections we make on history and the future, there is the personal, the voice which speaks from the *I* and remains alone within itself. Far easier is the discussion about civilization and history than what the *I* has to undertake to press its case for meaning and purpose. For this reason we produce more scholars who have learned to hide the self than thinkers who have cultivated it. When Senghor was asked the question: How do you now see your personal future? I felt that here was the test and I listened carefully to the reply. It was detailed and insightful. Senghor stated: "From my youth, from the benches at the lycée, and more exactly from Seminary Libermann, from where I felt – much more than conceived – Negritude I wanted to defend and illustrate my original civilization, that is, the spirit of this civilization: Negro African culture. At ten I would say I wanted to be a priest and professor. Today I want to be a man who has a simple obligation: to realize myself in a 'black Greece' [*Grèce noire*], bringing about the symbiosis of the values of Negritude and those of other civilizations."[6]

These remarks remain preliminary. There is the idea of a civilization of the universal which is the great light which makes us recall that beautiful line in Psalm 36: "In your light I see light." The *I* now speaks from the light that lights its soul, that gives birth to its faith and trust. Where this light dwells and surrounds its object, we discover the sources of the voice speaking through the *I*. Suddenly we realize that the personal *I* is our awareness of the divine speaking through us, animating our powers and showing us how intimate is our relationship to divinity.

"I wanted to be a poet," exclaimed Senghor, "in order to create, to give my people spiritual nourishment. We know that the great dream of the writer is to please his public. I am not an exception to the rule. My concern is less to have prizes – I have had many – than to have in my readers friends who, like me, with me, will find self-realization by fortifying themselves with spiritual nourishment. I have the impression that I have accomplished my task, my function as a poet."[7]

To be a poet is to have an obligation not only to the self but to a people and ultimately to mankind. The poet is the creator of "spiritual nourishment," he is the bringer of beauty, a being gifted with the power of the word. The poet is a maker whether he paints, writes, speaks; he is the inventor, the great transformer of life. In his hands, his words, his mind, the world is transfigured. This man not only invents, he converses

---

[6]Ibid., 344.
[7]Ibid.

with others, he reaches out to other peoples and civilizations and attempts to comprehend what men have done for millions, for thousands of years. Senghor thinks back to the Paleolithic Age, to a period when Africa was the avant-garde of civilization, to Egypt and the Middle East, to Sumerian writings, to the Indus valley and Davidian culture. He forms links which make us realize how diverse has been human civilization, what a mixture of peoples and cultures have flowed into each other and spread through the continents. However blurred this picture is, we know that being aware of our cultural diversity is the source of our conversations with both past and present. The ties to the past are fundamental for Senghor. From these we find inspirations, continuities, the sense of belonging which gives spiritual richness and beauty to life.

The *I* relates not only to the past and present, it speaks to the future. No one can leave Senghor without asking him if there is a message for those who wonder if just once again he will project his thoughts toward the future. To the final question concerning a message, Senghor replied: "This message, you have guessed it, is, above all else, a cultural one. Once again, the great debate of the last quarter of the twentieth century is neither political – dictatorship or democracy – nor economic – capitalism or socialism – but essentially cultural.... My message is that we must, first of all, be rooted in its [the twentieth century's] soul, its culture in order from there to assimilate, through ever-larger concentric circles, civilizations, other and different cultures."[8]

We listen to Senghor and his words become images. He awakens us to the vast cultural experiences which the world gives us. Always running away to the idols of the caves, to totems and taboos, we need to be drawn out of the caves toward the light of the sun. With Senghor, we walk from the cave in which we have dwelled. We need a companion to help us walk away from our fixed habits, to look in other directions, to hear new sounds and voices. Human creativity is a lonely affair. The *I* lives from the inspirations of others, from those about us, and those that speak to us from the past. The latter remain our fathers and to them we return again and again to hear the words and messages which we believe they have for us. In the solitude of creativity live the tranquil sounds that flow from secret and unexpected sources; they awaken us like the voice awakened Samuel. Their presence causes anxieties but slowly they become friendly and we accept them like the demon who is the reliable friend.

Senghor reminds us that his message is "that all of us – continents, races, nations, and civilizations – are embarked on the same destiny. It is not enough to say that on this great adventure we must necessarily be

[8]Ibid., 239.

firm. We must do more: cultivate our differences in order to enrich each other. Only in this way can we save ourselves or perish together. We save ourselves by creating a third way: the 'conciliatory accord' which will make us a greater man, a *greater being* in the core of the *Civilization of the Universal.*"[9]

We realize a powerful truth from these thoughts about Senghor. We are conscious of the *fact* that spiritual communication is conversational, that we are men because we converse with each other and can transcend the temporal and the spatial. We need our ancestors. We need to transform the present into visions of the future. We must overcome the confusion that lies in the differences between reality and ideality. If we are given the powers to believe in the future, we suddenly know that what is real is ideal, and the ideal is in its essence the real. Once we have seen the intimacy between reality and ideality, we realize that nothing is more vital to life than the presence of the ideal. It is to this presence that I have dedicated my conversations with Senghor. His life stretches through the ages. It is like the eternal book from which we have all drawn life. Whatever name this book takes through time, its fabric is woven by man's creative work, by his love of the divine, his adoration of his reason and his natural skills. Conversations with great souls draw us toward the miracles of the past, but also toward the wonders of the future. We see and hear both the pain and marvel of human life. We are dedicated to a continuity that has no beginning and possibly no end. We are men on a journey, called like Abraham from the land of his father to a new destiny, a new heroic vision of humankind.

---

[9]Ibid., 360.

2

The Embrace of Poetry and Science

Léopold Sédar Senghor is a poet who became a politician, a scholar, and a diplomat. He was a teacher and a war prisoner. In his noble tranquillity, he is a man of wisdom. He lived through the word that emerged from his African culture and from a civilization which he addressed in French. He was a poet who held before his people and the world a vision of an emerging humanity which needed and wanted the cultural contributions of all peoples. The poet whom Plato had expelled for falsity was in fact no poet. Senghor is the poet whom every culture proclaims as the singer of sacred incantations, the troubadour of noble dreams and verse, the creator of the vision which longs to be a dwelling in humanity. When once asked about the choice he would make if he could put aside his political responsibilities, he answered with powerful simplicity: poetry. "For me, if it were necessary to choose; what would you save from your triple life as political figure, professor, and poet? I always replied: My poems. They are essential. But what is the essence of this poetry which is the goal, the reason, and the essence of our lives? This is the second question, I do not say the most important. I speak of the concept before arriving at its expression; at its realization.[1]

Poetry is for Senghor a universal expression of man's creative experiences with the world and his tradition and his fellowmen. It belongs to the heritage of every cultural people who seek to find those necessary relationships which make life precious and meaningful. Poetry lives with the sanctity of the word of which no man can be deprived without lessening, and distorting, his humanity. It is the word that draws men to each other and allows them to find in it the original and unique experience that men have sought to develop with nature and divinity. We think of the Psalms, the odes of Pindar, of the epics of Homer and

[1]"Dialogue sur la poésie francophone," in *Oeuvre poétique* (Paris: Editions du Seuil, 1990), 377-78.

Virgil, and through Senghor of the poetry of Africa, and we realize how precious the word has been, is, and will be for men in search of the symbols of mankind. The word is sacred and it has been rightly identified with God. It is a truth that no man dominates; it remains a veil, a mist, which only the poet and the painter allow us to experience; it is a sacred door before which a man stands, but no man enters. If no man enters, but man believes that there is a truth, then it is the poet who dreams of the truth, proclaims its existence, and forces man to struggle to lift the veils that conceal the truth. Like the poets, the philosophers were lovers who needed their demons, who learned the powers of sacred initiations and the marvels of incantations. Each poet and philosopher heard the voice of a Diotima which showed him his childishness, and taught him to pose the questions of truth. Senghor is a teacher not only in Africa and France, but to all men who would listen and realize that the poet was not a mere juggler of verse, a craftsman of the word, a giver of pleasure, but a thinker, a painter of symbols and signs, a hearer whose intuition brought him close to the divine word.

The poet did not emerge suddenly. Poetry appeared to him in boyhood and remained embodied in his soul, growing and developing in travel, education, politics, and scholarship. There were men whose formidable intellect deeply impressed Senghor. Fellow contemporary poets like Pierre Emmanuel, Jean-Claude Renard, Alain Bosquet are his companions, sharing a political-philosophical view of the power and precocity of the word, imagining a "world capital of poetry." There were poets who also developed their visions in prose, who gave poetry a universal content through images and myths, men of hope and inspiration. The man from whom few sensitive souls could escape was the Jesuit Pierre Teilhard de Chardin, poet and scientist, visionary and believer.

The name of Teilhard appears again and again in the writings of Senghor. If we read through the essays included in *Liberté*, volume 3, *Négritude et Civilization de l'Universel* (Liberty, volume 3, Negritude and Civilization of the Universal), Teilhard is often there to remind us of the deep and intimate relationship between them. But it was to a conference devoted to Teilhard in 1961, six years after his death, that Senghor sent a long and detailed lecture on the significance of Teilhard's philosophy. Senghor could not attend the conference at Vézelay; he was in Madagascar attending a conference of the Assembly of French-speaking African States. The aim of the conference at Vézelay was to encourage the nations to develop their moral, religious, and cultural values. Only this development would make it possible for them to face the future of an emerging mankind. "The day when all nations take this path, humanity will be mature and form efficaciously its unity."[2] These words of purpose were fundamental and precious to both Teilhard and Senghor. They struggled for that heart-to-heart contact between peoples, which alone could make the future of humankind a possibility.

The world of Teilhard was happily not discussed by a fellow cleric, scholar, or philosopher, but by a poet from a continent unknown to vast numbers of educated men. The perspective had changed, no more dabblings in theological and theoretical niceties, no more searches for orthodoxies, and no more attempts at subtleties that would turn the ambiguous into the unambiguous, the unclear into the clarified. Senghor found in Teilhard a thinker who could speak the dreams and visions of his poetry, the longing he had to find a place for every distinct and unique culture in a world where he and Teilhard believed that man was essentially the same no matter where he was found. To an Africa that sought its place in humankind, Teilhard offered a view of universality that rejected what was static and defined. He revealed a "holy evolution" which gave place and value to every living whole. He did not judge cultures as higher and lower, conferring upon some the accolades of reason and rejecting in others the arbitrariness of sentimentality. He recognized the differences in development. He sought the unique and the value of its expression. He envisioned the end of isolation and disdain, finding new depths of emotion, new myths and images of man's relationship to the world and to God. Here lay the overwhelming problem of communication, the study of languages and literature, music and art. Here lay a study that would be more than academic, that yearned to discover new dimensions of the human reality, new perspectives on the human character, and a renewed feeling for the infinite quality of creativity. It is this last quality that is vital to man, to the discoveries which he must constantly make to find ways to realize the capacities for work which lie within him.

Senghor began his address with a reminder of how scandalous it seemed in 1937 at Dakar when he spoke of the need "to return to the sources," to the vernacular languages. "Such was the degradation to be found in the 'black soul,'" he stated, "that we accepted being a 'tabula rasa,' a race, almost a continent which for 30,000 years had thought nothing, felt nothing, written nothing, painted, sculptured, sung, and danced nothing. A nothingness [*unnéant*] at the bottom of the abyss, which knew only how to implore and receive, a softened wax in the hands of the white God with pale pink fingers and sky blue eyes."[3]

---

[2]"Pierre Teilhard et la politique africaine," in *Cahier: Pierre Teilhard de Chardin* (Paris: Editions du Seuil, 1962), 12.
[3]Ibid., 17.

Senghor had no doubt that his continent needed Europe, and in particular France, to force it to think about itself, to begin that precious reflection which all peoples must experience to realize their dependence both upon themselves and upon others. Here emerges the first and primordial of all realities: mutual spiritual and physical dependence. All men find within their societal myths moments of chosenness and moments of mutuality. Senghor needed the spirit of France. His Africa needed her.

France, who could give much, also needed Africa. She needed those who came to her for all sorts of skills, for education and conversation. This France needed to be called upon and summoned to be a partner with the peoples she had conquered and who now wanted to live as equals with her. Here begins that process from which humankind emerges, that feeling that peoples are contributors to each other, essential elements in all cultural achievements. The dreamers need to find ways to the idea of civilization; to search in the evolution of cultural dependencies for convergence and coreflection.

Senghor did not hesitate to say: "I repeat it, it is Europe, France who saved us. They did this by developing in us a *reflection* [*réflexion*] supported by the facts and their *comprehension* [*compréhension*], and auto-criticism and above all, by teaching us the values of black Africa.... It is Europe – such is the dialectic of life – France who would make us discover the values of Negritude *activating* in us, to speak like Teilhard de Chardin, with the powers of the heart, the powers of *reflection: coreflection* [*coréflexion*]."[4] In these hopes and desires lives the tragedy of humankind. We know how deeply we need other peoples and cultures, how dependent we are upon them, but we also know that every human creation is fallible and inadequate, morally compromised and compromising. Peoples have suffered from the weaknesses of racism, and nationalism, from a demonic sense of self-sufficiency and deified glory. But the overriding reality is the interrelationships that grow among peoples who are not weakened by moral deficiencies, but find their truth in themselves and in others.

Senghor spoke of Negritude, which he defined as "*the assembly of the values of civilization of the black world.* It is not racism, it is *culture*. It is *a situation understood* and controlled in order to apprehend the cosmos by being in accord with it.... Negritude was intuitive reason, the embracing reason; it was not the eye of reason. To be precise, it was the *communal warmth, the image-symbol and the cosmic rhythm which did not sterilize by dividing, but nourished by uniting*."[5] To relate to the world, Senghor knew

---

[4]Ibid., 18, 19.
[5]Ibid., 20.

that Africa must first discover herself, know herself, and reflect upon the meaning of this knowledge. He realized that in a European world that gave birth to Nazism, Fascism, and Communism, there were truths to be learned for Africa. These European diseases knew no borders and easily traversed the seas. Africa could receive them with ease and pleasure. "The triumph of Nazis and the Second World War," he said, "sobered us. We finally understood that racism was hate and violence. The *war* became planetary because of the new weapon of destruction. Science was put in the service of Death, not in that of Life. We had become aware that racial purity was a false myth. From the Neolithic period, races hardly as yet formed, had begun to mix. The first civilizations of the Nile, the Euphrates, of the Indus, were mixed civilizations (*métisses*),the common work of black and white peoples. They were doublessly successful."[6]

If racial purity was a false myth, then it was necessary to search in the tradition for one that would liberate man. It was not surprising that Senghor, like most intellectuals, found his vision in Marxism, but not in Leninism. "Marxism," he noted, "was going to be our first instrument of liberation."[7] This was a Marxism which expanded the idealism of the French Revolution, which reduced the philosophical ideas of contradictions to laws of historical development and finally found a way to identify the dialectics of nature with laws of necessity. Senghor wanted to see in Marxism the alienation of man from the products and pleasures of his work, an alienation which revealed oppression, and condemned capitalism to forms of tyranny. Setting forth an identification between capitalism and oppression, Marxism created the myth of class liberation. Senghor realized that in order to waken "the world of energies," myth was the primordial tool. "It was necessary," he explained, "to abandon the negative attitude. Not by letting History be made, but by positively *making History ourselves*, by conforming it to *Nature*."[8] Marxism had become the myth of the French intellectuals in the 1930s, but it was tempered by Senghor with the search for freedom and individual rights. Senghor appreciated in it the struggle to overcome the persistent alienation that lay at the foundation of human society. He believed that this struggle needed more than class antagonism, the claims of inevitability, the victorious march of the working class. Marxism had to be tempered by personalism, the work of the journal *Esprit* and its editor Emmanuel Mounier. But the strongest complementary force to Marxism was Teilhard and his belief in the

---

[6]Ibid., 21.
[7]Ibid.
[8]Ibid.

spiritual dimension of man's experience, the idea of evolution, the expanding universe, and a deepened faith in God.

Senghor found in Marx not only the teacher of political economy, but the founder of a humanism which belonged to the concrete relationships of man in an industrial society: alienation, surplus value, historical evolution, myth. In clear and precise words, Senghor stated: "The essential merit of Marx is not to have taught political economy – but *Humanism,* to have revealed to us man in and beyond economic *History,* concrete man with material and spiritual needs, his alienations, struggles, and his future triumph in the rediscovery of freedom. He defined for us his aim: 'to penetrate the real and intimate whole of the relationships of production in bourgeois society,' 'to unveil the economic law of movement in modern society.' In this sense, Marx is the founder of Sociology, that is, of modern Humanism."[9]

If we think of the impact of Marx after the death of Hegel, of the meaningless disputes over the meaning and intention of Hegel's philosophy, of the divisions of the philosophy into left-wing and right-wing Hegelians, we realize how original was Marx's understanding of the implication of Hegel's *Philosophy of Law.* Senghor found a philosophical tradition that belonged to the marketplace. He could understand the needs of Africa in terms of the haves and have-nots, the exploited and the exploiters. In fact, the Marx that Senghor took from the tradition was the Marx he needed and used. The poet had come to the sociologist for language and myth, for a sense of history and a construct of nature. He found enough to satisfy his wants. He needed to know only the Marx of his imagination. If against this Marx, Senghor placed Teilhard, it was not as if two antagonists would fight to the death. "I repeat," Senghor said, "it would be an error to think that [Teilhard] held Marx in disdain. To be sure, Marx was for him an adversary. He was not an enemy. He was the only adversary worthy of confrontation. He said this on many occasions."[10]

Senghor had divided his contribution to the conference into three parts: Negritude and Marxism, Pierre Teilhard de Chardin or Cohesion, and Fecundity and Negritude as the African Way of Socialism. When he turned directly to Teilhard, he mentioned that his discussion centered on three volumes of Teilhard's complete works: volume 2, *The Appearance of Man*; volume 3, *The Vision of the Past;* volume 5, *The Future of Man.*

As we move from Marx to Teilhard, we are confronted by a new and novel phenomenon: the planetary phenomenon. Man is no longer an economic, sociological, or political being, he is now a "cosmic

---

[9]Ibid., 23.
[10]Ibid., 33-34.

phenomenon," and it is this vision that becomes the dominant one in Senghor's image of reality. Suddenly, the relationship has shifted from Africa and Europe to the universe in which the latter has a place among infinite groups of cultural realities. Sociology, philosophy, poetry, ethnology, paleontology join to bring forth a universal view of man's place in the cosmos. Evolution is no longer limited to biology. Man is liberated from all static concepts, religion is making us more and more aware that the divine is beyond the dogmas in which we have imprisoned it to satisfy our limited imagination.

The majesty of divinity is emerging through the wonders and marvels of an expanding universe and consciousness. We realize that it is the future that holds the realization of humankind. The latter has only just begun to be conceived and comprehended. There is an exciting optimism in the future possibilities of man and universe that come forth not only from man, but from God. The pain and disasters that confront us in daily life are not the ultimate realities, although they appear to be such. There is an evolution that is taking place *in spite of* what occurs about us. It is in this evolution that we discover the hints of the divine, that allows and forces us to look ahead, in belief and trust, to a universe that is incomplete and yet divine, that has only begun to reveal its truth to man and universe.

What is striking and deeply significant is Senghor's acceptance of God. This Point Omega is the force that draws reality toward itself. "This attracting center, this *Point Omega*," Senghor stated, "is nothing other than *God*. Thus, God appears logically rather than *dialectically* at the end of the cosmic and human movement."[11] What does this imply for those who believe that the Revelation was totally given? Each generation turns back, in memory, to Sinai and Horeb, to the birth, life, and death of the Christ. Each attempts to absolutize the reality that has broken into time and space and brought forth a new history, a new vision, and an embracing love. The static quality of the Revelation is broken. Its fixity yields to a cosmic growth and development. From the human perspective, the realization of divinity is in evolution, giving more and more testimony to man's spiritual powers. These are being brought forth through the attracting powers of God which have only just begun to fill the universe and man with their efficacious and nourishing powers. Man seems to have only begun his journey toward the divine. He has taken his first steps in reflection. What he has confessed in faith is the wonder of the veil behind which there are greater and deeper abysses to ponder. God has allowed man to begin his journey. What was so striking for Senghor was the *fact* that this journey, being taken by humankind, is

---

[11]Ibid., 52.

reaching out to higher and profounder syntheses, exploring new and novel realms of spiritual possibilities. This movement of humankind is no longer a European or Asian monopoly. It demands the efforts of the universe in which every culture has a role, and in which every culture has a future part to play.

Senghor discovered in Teilhard the essentiality of movement. Distinct from all secular humanisms that never went beyond the autonomy of the individual and, often, a deification of man, was Teilhard's faith in the attracting "pull" of God. Here we touch on a mystery and marvel that link the secular and divine in such a way that the distinction fades away, and we realize how receptive matter is to the divine. It awaits it in longing and hope. Matter is potentially spirit. God is not that static other, the unapproachable Deity above the universe that sits in judgment and allows it to spin out its destiny. God is in the universe. He has created it, draws from it the forces that yearn for him and his love. His love animates and causes motion, those undetermined drifts and jolts toward higher syntheses. Mystery lies in these drifts from above and from below, from the knowledge that the divine in infinite ways infuses a matter that is not indifferent, but receptive to the light that falls upon it, waiting, as it were, for the source of its reality. Man is the mediator between light and matter attempting to find the awareness that everything and everyone is changing and evolving. These drifts and jolts are not determined by an inscrutable law of nature; rather, chance and contingency are always present and prevalent in all material and human actions. What is radically startling is the movement from above, the divine action upon the universe. If Senghor felt that Marx was fulfilled by Teilhard, he meant that Teilhard had discovered that other dimension of reality: the flow from the above. How do we know this? We have no answer; we have only a belief that emerges from experience, from the creative act, from the vision we have of the growing universe.

Senghor described these movements. He remarked: "The sole thought, the single style of invention, the *external push* do not suffice to cause Humanity to advance toward the Finality which we have discovered. We must add a powerful *attraction* as Teilhard said. There must be a *pull* at the same time as the *push*. We must cultivate 'the forces of Finality,' the forces of Liberty, which alone give us the possibility of 'transhumanizing' ourselves through 'coalescence' and 'combining conspiration.'"[12] For Senghor, this was more than a scientific or a poetic vision. It was the creation of the religious, which had regained its ancient right as a creator of myths and maker of reality. The religious-poetic held forth the image, the destiny, the subtle interrelationships which linked

---

[12]Ibid., 54.

matter and spirit in a ladderlike movement. Man must learn to dream. This is now the message of the poet. This dream is the light of a universe that needs courage and new ways of thought for its architecture. The old philosophies are over, the openness of man's soul leads to new discoveries and relationships. Man is incomplete. All that is around him searches to receive what will open and reveal the future. The future is the realm of the possible, the unexpected and unknown. These are not vague illusions, but the reality that comes from the awareness of the divine presence, that miraculous "pull" that draws everything from the egoistic self, the consciousness that the divine is active, and moves us in ways that man experiences as marvels and wonders. The majestic presence of divinity fills the universe in infinite forms and forces us to realize that God is everywhere, moving all this in divine evolution.

The question that presses upon us again and again concerns the "*forces of Finality*." "They are the *values* of Philosophy," Senghor stated, "which are values only because they are instruments of Finality, instruments of our *transhumanization*. They are the currents of that coreflection which we have spoken about. We consider them as the consequences, the external push of coreflection."[13] Why does Senghor feel so close to Teilhard, to his language and thought? There are no conclusive answers to this question; there are feelings and undefined attachments, sympathies and undisclosed identifications. Teilhard had broken away from the European philosophers. He gave those who lived in other continents the possibility of seeing themselves as parts of a universal movement, of a planetary reality that had a unique place for them in a whole embodied in God. Men are infinite possibilities, cosmic phenomena, belonging to a universe that is in the process of creating persistently new forms of reality, new dimensions of intelligence, new powers of the imagination. Men have to learn that what bends them to each other is not only the earth but the spirit. There is a common destiny that depends upon the uniqueness of every cultural form. There is this embracing coreflection that reveals to every society the spiritual and physical dependence that leads to their evolution. The poet always knows that men must learn again how to imagine and envision the truth that is always present and is dwelling among them.

Life takes on a profound value. It is lived not only for self-enjoyment, but for its capacity to do, to create, and to give unending possibilities of forms and colors to the imagination. Life becomes an awakening to a world of energies which we have only just begun to envisage. There is a spiritual and physical excitement that accompanies our awareness that we have only just begun to explore the energies that are in life. With this

---

[13]Ibid., 54.

awareness, life becomes a reality we not only respect but love. We feel its wonder in the contributions of people who live with us, people we have never known nor attempted to comprehend. We realize that life is being created through unending architectural forms in places that remain to us unknown and unexplored. We are aware that wherever there are men there are the arts in every imaginable form. Men have sought them from their minds and their hands, in their voices and their incantations, in their dances and myths. There is an irreversible and immortal movement flowing through humankind. Sadly, we remain restricted to that element of it which we were taught at birth to respect. What was different and unknown was foreign and untouchable. Senghor had an unexplored culture to bring to Europe, to make it palpable and appreciated by cultures convinced of their own superiority and their mission to civilize the rest of mankind. Senghor knew that Europe had an indispensable science which had to be learned in Africa, but Africa had much to teach to the Europeans. Here begin the conversations, the formations of perspective and intimate relationships that develop between people who know that they must learn from each other. Senghor loved France, the country of poets and artists, political thinkers and philosophers, the nation formed in Revolution and alive with revolutionary hope and vision. But there was Africa, Senegal, and in her there was also thought, art and poetry, dance and social order. Senghor was beyond this "trade balance." He envisioned a universe in which God drew forth the elements and energies of all peoples. This "pull" he learned to love.

Every thinker, particularly the one who has assumed political office – Senghor was president of Senegal from 1960-80 – needs a dream to confront the reality that he finds before him daily. Man is the only being who needs to create a reality beyond what he encounters. He needs the future to make the present and past endurable. This necessity is as demanding as the physical satisfactions of everyday life. Human life is inseparable from the question of its significance. Man is the only being who exclaims: What does it all mean? whose prayers are filled with questions of good and evil, suffering and its justification. Man has created a Job, a monument to his search for values and the purposefulness of life. He is the only being who assumes for himself the right to question God.

In this inquisitive soul lies man's realization that there is a truth beyond the reconciliations, compromises, solutions which he requires for his way through daily life. Senghor noted that "behind racial, national, religious hates, the international tensions which we experience presently, are the painful acts of giving birth to the planetary civilization. This civilization will only be achieved again at the last stage of the panhuman convergence *in* and *by* the Love of the *Superperson*. Only the *Person itself*, through the reciprocal love which it exercises on individuals, draws them into his heart and personalizes them. Only the *Center* itself, by effecting the synthesis of the innumerable particular centers which are fulfilled in it, achieves them. Thus, at this last critical point, Humanity, through a final jolt, leaps out of Space-Time. This has always been the dream of Man."[14]

Here we touch upon the most significant reality in this universal planetary conception. We speak of the "jolt." The jolt gives a precious indeterminism to all that occurs and will happen. There is no foretelling; there is only chance and possibility. The vision of Senghor is founded upon a holy evolution that embraced those precious jolts which make a mockery of all determinisms seeking to incarcerate man and humankind in the laws invented by the intellect. Without the predictable movements governing the universe, without the permanency of time and space, we can assume the possibility of an as-yet-unimagined relationship between man and the world. The vision belongs to men who are capable of reflecting upon the future, of comprehending growth and progress in new ways and forms, and who are willing to recognize the divinity as the universal love which draws everything toward itself. What has fallen away is the notion that progress is a determined and orderly development, and what we have discovered are the drifts and sways, jolts and pulls. We have lost our futile attempt to dominate the universe. We yield to God and we seek again to discover the meaning of his love, the powers of his attractions. We have returned to the primordial vision of wonder and marvel, to the openness of the soul, to revelation that has not only happened, but is occurring persistently, forcing us to realize that neither man nor universe are finished realities.

Senghor realized that any universal planetary system must bear within it a discussion of human freedom. The freedom of the individual has its limits, but also its responsibilities that are not static; like the universe, this freedom changes and develops. "The individual," Senghor reminded us, "is realized as person only through freedom. Because the movement itself being here, by its attraction gives a style of life and action: going forward into the meaning of the current – A freedom taken in isolation is weak and uncertain and can easily wander away into gropings."[15] Freedom depends upon belonging, upon the assumption of obligation, but, above all, freedom is the capacity which makes it possible for us to be open to new ideas and aspirations. Man learns to aspire to more than his welfare; he longs for the greater being (*le plus être*). This longing can be accomplished only on a planetary level, in the

---

[14]Ibid., 57.
[15]Ibid., 60-61.

realm of a deeper socialization, with a dependence that is not only economic and technical but spiritual and religious. We have gone far beyond the Marxism which Senghor appreciated and which he believed Teilhard complemented and fulfilled. Senghor's mention of Marxism seems antiquated as he moves deeply into the spiritual world of Teilhard. There he found a true dwelling for the poet-thinker. The search for and affirmation of *le plus être* is decisive. Man's reality is less in the world of the concrete than in that of the idea, in the loving God who embraces all that is real: the holy evolution of humankind.

What excites Senghor in his relationship to Teilhard is the realization that Teilhard reawakens in him the "world of energies." A vision emerges, man is jolted from that static world of fixed truths, laws, categories, from the limits of time and space and the limited concepts that emerges from them. This excitement has political and social consequences. Given forms are not absolute, the presence of the divine assures the universe of progress and change and these cannot be predetermined; they belong to the unexpected, the unknown, and the ambiguous. God is not in history; he is the Beyond, the Point Omega, but he affects history and draws it toward the timeless and spaceless. Senghor knew that every reality was touched by this divine presence; every being and culture has a place in it. Man needs to learn a new humanism, a cosmic and planetary one. With these new dimensions, every element has a contributory role and man seeks to understand the peculiar and distinct place that belongs to it. Aware that he will be forever unsuccessful in his search for totality, he turns with openness and imagination to the embracing powers of the future. In these lie the inscrutable possibilities that come forth so unexpectedly from every form of expression and productivity. Every people is at the service of humanity, every creation belongs both to the particular and the universal. We are beyond the European ideologies of the nineteenth and twentieth centuries, beyond Marxism, materialism, liberalism, not to mention the distortions of racism, nationalism, statism. Poetry and philosophy demand new dimensions, universal and planetary ones, to realize that man is beyond group, nation, and continent. Senghor noted that "socialism is henceforth defined for us as *the method which puts economic, political, social, and cultural research and techniques in the service of the panhuman socialization*, that is, the civilization of the Universal. *This is the Humanism of contemporary times.*"[16]

It was the future that drove man from the imprisonment of the present and the past. What man considers to be real, what occurs about him daily, is not the only or even the essential reality. The future is an

---

[16]Ibid., 63.

imposing power, it gives new dimensions to life; it forces us to rethink the present, to question its encompassing domination. Teilhard stated that "the world will belong tomorrow to those who will bring to the earth, that is, from this earth, a greater hope."[17] Teilhard brought Senghor a faith that was "supremely futuristic." Moralism and legalism are the rules of the present; they are the foundations of every justifiable society. Their strength depends upon man's sensitivity to human dignity and the rights flowing from it. Religion was born in the promise of the future, in the sublimity of the rainbow, the trust in the Covenant, that alliance between God and man, between the divine and the universe. The divine presence is the source of man's hope, the future is that presence, the reality of his kingdom. Knowing that it is present liberates man and nature from the determinism of fate and the cyclical movement of time.

No doctrine is more expressive of the absence of God than the belief in cyclical time. Neither hope nor love break through this cyclic flow, only the God of Revelation. The Sublime Attraction is the future. The faith that it necessitates revolutionizes the universe. Divine love draws all reality toward its Presence. It reveals the possibility of the unexpected and unknown energy alive in Being. From it comes the jolt that is in every act of creativity. Nothing is predictable and determined. There is no fate.

Janet G. Vaillant, in her distinguished biography of Senghor, speaks of the thinkers who nourished Senghor's thinking, his search for a philosophy of personalism, and his rejection of materialism. No philosophy could have a meaning for him that did not embrace the future and did not comprehend man's tie to that divine awakening of the energies of the world. "He had found," Vaillant writes, "[this congeniality] among his French contemporaries of the interwar period, who attacked French materialism and the dehumanization and conformity of modern industrial life, in a particularly congenial form among such Catholic thinkers as Paul Claudel, Jacques Maritain and Emmanuel Mounier with his theory of personalism and sensitivity to the spiritual poverty of French life.... And finally in his reading of the remarkable Jesuit philosopher Teilhard de Chardin, Senghor had found the promise that the world was evolving toward a point where man would be restored to his totality and love would harmonize all human differences. The positive goals of these Catholic thinkers and their determination to find ways to restore the primacy of the human

[17]Ibid., 97.

personality and community, fit well with Senghor's vision of the values to be found in African societies."[18]

Where the philosophers gathered there were also the poets, there were his friends Pierre Emmanuel, Alain Bosquet, Jean-Claude Renard. Here the philosophers gathered, there the poets. We turn from one to the other, hoping we could say let's stop here and cease our visits; but alas, this will never happen. If Teilhard was unique in giving to poets and philosophers a vision, then wherever we go among them we enter a world of images, metaphors, and imagination. Freed from the atheism of materialism and the fate of cyclical movement, we join the poets. We search with them for the love and attachment binding them to Senghor, telling the philosophers that soon we will come to them to understand their influence on our poet and thinker.

Teilhard brought something unique and sublime to Senghor. He brought that distinct union of science and philosophy. He brought the powers of the imagination which tie the endeavors of humankind in a sacred community, drawing to it the imaginative work of all men. This community is the capital of humankind to which the poet offers his incantations, and the philosopher his imagery. Where we find the philosopher, we also discover the poet, and where the latter speaks, the minds of the philosophers hover about and listen.

---

[18]*Black, French, and African: A Life of Léopold Sédar Senghor* (Cambridge: Harvard University Press, 1990), 261.

3

Priest, Poet, Scientist: Pierre Teilhard de Chardin

There emerges in every great life a belief which slowly and continuously draws it from immediate and habitual concerns, and forces it to recognize the fact that it is governed and controlled by a reality greater than the self. In whatever direction we turn, we find that men, in all parts of the world, feel compelled to find some identification with what they have acknowledged as traditional faiths, moral and legal attitudes. There are others who have lived with ancient traditions and feel the discomforts of their forms. They find it difficult to hear the voices that speak through them. These men know that there are truths beyond those that have been spoken and heard, that there is a growing awareness that enhances spiritual and material life, and that divinity is more than a fixed and defined reality.

Philosophers have called for a courageous philosophy. Scientists have experienced the wonders of an expanding universe. Theologians have sought with care and conviction to deepen our consciousness of God, and to expand our vision of a universe that has thrown aside its given shackles and revealed to us its sense of sublimety and beauty. We could speak of revolutionary forces animating our spiritual and physical existence. These forces found dynamic and courageous expression in Pierre Teilhard de Chardin (1881-1955), a rare and beautiful Jesuit priest whose life journeyed from science, to poetry, to a peculiar and distinct literature which flows from those in whom wonder creates language and vision. In wonder, as the ancients taught, the greatness of the human soul finds its source. It is in this phenomenon of wonder that the soul begins its way through life, and gives it meaning and purpose.

We turn toward the world and man with an intuitive interest, with the feeling that we are involved not only with the enhancement of our societal and natural life, but with the divine reality. We believed that there is a divine force above and beyond us that set us forth on our natural journey, watches over us in a fatherly way, and judges the right and wrong we do to each other. Yet in every great believer there lived a unique spiritual experience, a loneliness that separated him from those about him, that brought him close to the divine, and made him anxiously aware that he shared a divine destiny, that he belonged to others in a rare and penetrating way. Teilhard knew what this experience was, he lived it in a vision as unique and startling as that which came upon spiritual explorers and makers who see in themselves and in the distance the wonders that have attracted and nourished them. The wonder never falls prey to the need for definition and fixity. It entices and allures. It creates the inspiration and love that molds and constructs the work that longs for the spirit. The creator needs, Teilhard stated, "to penetrate the beautifying value and the eternal hopes of the holy Evolution. That is the word that I desire, above all others, to make heard. It is the one that reconciles God and the World."[1]

Here Teilhard links two words that we would hold apart. With great audaciousness they are brought together, in violation of tradition, which knows the incommensurability of the one with the other. We find it difficult to avoid thinking of everything about us in static and definable terms. We have become habituated to the distinct and limited quality in which we dwell, in which we seek the securities of our thinking and acting. Evolution is more than biological change, mutations of species. It is the realization that there are vast developments taking place within the universe and these are being fed by forces that not only proceed from natural changes, but are drawn forth by divine power. Not only what comes forth from the earth is involved, but what waters it, what comes forth from the heavens and nourishes it.

We know that the universe is filled with forces with which we have not as yet made contact, forces that are beyond our spiritual capacities, and which await our growth and development. The divine which draws us from the limitations of the self, from the individuality in which we sought to discover the complexities of spiritual life, is similarly undergoing enhancement and growth. From the human perspective, the divine awaits to be revealed to man and the world. What we believe has come forth in given revelations is made possible by our capacity of receptivity. We can, however, no longer receive as an individual. We have learned to be receptive as a member of a believing community. Teilhard remarked: "There was, perhaps, a time before our own when individuals could still try to better themselves and fulfill themselves,

[1]Pierre Teilhard de Chardin, *Écrits du temps de la guerre, 1916-1919* (Paris: Editions du Seuil, 1965), 22.

each on his own, in isolation. The time has gone forever. We now have to make up our minds to recognize that at no moment in history has man been so completely involved (both actively and passively) through the very foundations of his being, in the value and betterment of all those around him, as he is today. And all the evidence indicates that this regime of interdependence can only become more pronounced in the course of the coming centuries."[2]

The individual discovers his reality in the community, which embraces the human species with forms and traditions. The discovery of community does not destroy the individual, who finds the sacredness of his being in a reality that is more and more permeated with divinity. The community of mankind bears within it an incommunicable power which unites all beings in a dimension where they discover what is unique in all beings. It is this uniqueness that links them with the divine, that makes them aware of the spirit and matter that belong to each other, and that they have not only an earthly destiny, but one that is divine. Sacredness dwells in the inseparability of movements and beings. In every aspect of cosmic existence there are ties to others. The religious feeling, the intuitive reason that is its power, belong to this grasp of interrelationship which makes each reality a part of another, each growth and enhancement a reflection and participant in others.

Teilhard noted that "man is essentially the same in all of us, and we have only to look sufficiently deeply within ourselves to find a common substratum of aspirations and illuminations. To put it in a way which already expresses my fundamental thesis: 'It is through that which is most incommunicably personal in us that we make contact with the universal.'"[3]

We are beyond analytical biology and sociology. We speak of a growing universe in which man is reaching new levels of awareness, where he is exploring and discovering the divinity that lies in him, the nourishment that feeds and illuminates him. We are on the threshold of seeing the collapse of a fixed and definitional world. We are observing the emergence of a universe in which the mutuality of relationships between community and divinity is becoming increasingly apparent. We comprehend that this relationship is born in faith, in a reality that grows from itself, from its capacity to grasp the depths of the faith which lives in others, in the knowledge that faith engenders fidelity as spirit engenders imagination. But what we discover in our faith, our fidelity to

---

[2]"The Evolution of Responsibility in the World," in *Activation of Energy* (New York: Harcourt Brace Jovanovich, 1970), 212.

[3]How I Believe (New York: Harper & Row, 1969), 12. *Comment je crois,* in *Oeuvres de Pierre Teilhard de Chardin* (Paris: Editions du Seuil, 1969), see 10:117-152.

the world, is the attraction of God. This attraction is the wonder we discover in the growth and progress about us. God is that evolution to which all reality adheres and from which it grows.

Above and beyond our faith in God and in the spirit is our love of the world. This is the most difficult love. It is the love that is most deeply challenged and denied by what we see and experience, by what we call evil. Yet it is this love that most deeply challenges our fidelity. We are drawn to the world by our needs and satisfactions. We long to satisfy them, but the world is more than the source of our pleasures. It embodies life, a growth and a development. In it, each reality and people discover that they are contributors with unique possibilities and aptitudes. From all parts of the universe, the call is heard to bring forth the culture and history that belong to each individual part. A vision emerges that allows us to see beyond the distortions and dismemberments which we call evil, which allows us to comprehend in new and novel ways the varied levels of spiritual life. Knowing what we must struggle against makes it possible for us to know what battle we have to fight, and which is worthy of our sacrifice and our life. We cry out for peace, but this peace is not a fixed reality but one that is balanced with struggle and contradiction. Order lives with conflict. Opposites belong to each other in a balance that is beautiful. Where the opposites fade away, their place is taken by one dominant form. Man loses the sense of an evolving universe progressing from order to conflict and again to order.

We call a philosophy courageous that seeks universality. Philosophy desires to find not only a theory of knowledge, of ethics or aesthetics, but also one that goes forth from faith that proceeds from the world and that comes down upon it from the divine. To acknowledge a world filled with forces that we have as yet not explored is to comprehend that wonder which Aristotle taught was the beginning of thinking, He understood the essence of a courageous philosophy. In our time this was clearly enunciated by the Jerusalem philosopher Hugo Bergman. Teilhard directed us to this path, but like all others, he found a mankind unprepared for his vision. This vision opens to us the movements of the incredible realities that fill our universe, that link humanity and divinity and make it possible for us to envision a humankind that bears within it wonders that have yet to be fathomed, sublimities that await our perceptions. These will not come forth with ease and pleasure. They will foster struggle and contradiction, but with fidelity to the world, we know that they will emerge, giving us a deeper insight into what we call the divine. No longer is the divine fixed to a *here* and *now*, or to a *there* and an *above*. The divine unfolds through our heightened sense of understanding, realizing that our physical and spiritual evolution have only just begun, like the Greek philosophers who in their restless search for first principles sought to find that implosive force that links the heavens and the earth.

Teilhard knew that even if he were to lose his faith in a personal God, he would never yield his fidelity to the world. "I feel," he stated, "that I should continue *to believe* invincibly *in the world.* The world (its value, its infallibility and its goodness) when all is said and done, is the first, the last, and the only thing in which I believe. It is by this faith that I live. And it is to this faith, I feel, that at the moment of death, rising above all doubts, I shall surrender myself."[4] We ask in amazement, who speaks with these words? Is it the Jesuit priest, the scientist, the thinker, or are they all speaking the same love of creation that comes with the love of the divine? All the forces of life and thought speak in and from Teilhard as they speak in every great being who has become aware that the separations we have made and fostered through the generations can no longer be worthy of our rationality and feeling. What we have held apart in our search for purity and limitation belong together. They are not identical, but they are inseparable, at times estranged from each other, but never irreconcilable. Fidelity to the earth reflects our love of the emerging and unifying differentiations that reveal the sublimity and beauty of the world. We speak not only of man, but of all organic and inorganic life forms. Fidelity to this earth is faith in God, the Point Omega of all reality, that sacred attraction that moves all worldly forms and shows us how they share with each other that evolution of the universe.

Faith in the world makes it possible for us to extend our being, to deepen our vision, to be faithful to a universe that grows, that impels the imagination to go beyond its immediate limits, and to know that there is a divine spirit that infuses all that is. Religion can no longer be for us a historical event or action, unless we are able to see in it the symbols of a reality that is yet to appear as we grow in feeling, knowledge, and imagination. Religion is faith in the sacredness of growth and development. It is the consciousness of the infinite possibilities which we have called the believing community. This community is no longer a historical and designated group, but it bears within it the contributions of the human cultures that have grown on the continents and among its peoples. We learn to see in each a divine moment searching for realization. No longer do we limit the divine to one people, one religion, but we see in all cultures divine chosenness. Each people speaks of its divinity. Each can do this because of its uniqueness. This uniqueness links group to group. Only in it is each being prepared for faith in the

---

[4]Ibid., 19-20.

divine; only in it does each being seek to find that "cosmic sense" that balances individuality and universality.

We could say that "we used to look upon ourselves and the things around us as 'points' closed in on themselves. We now see things as threadless fibers, woven into a universal process. Everything falls back into a past abyss, and everything rushes forward into a future abyss. Through its history, every being is co-extensive with the whole of duration; and its ontogenesis is no more than the infinitesimal element of a cosmogenesis, in which is ultimately expressed the individuality – the face, we might say – of the universe."[5]

With the limitation of the closed universe, with the mysterious sense of growth and development being revealed to us, we feel not only a liberation from traditional forms, but an openness to the varied aspects of life and beliefs that inhabit humankind. These make us aware that the forms we have lived with and grown used to are distinct to a particular way of life, and that there are other expressions and values that have significance and purpose. We become deeply conscious of a dependence on others and their contributions; we feel that there is a life that permeates all human forms which peoples have formed and molded in different ways. In each there lie a divine sign and symbol that make it possible for us to learn its truth. There lies a peculiar greatness in that individual for whom the multiplicity of forms is a genuine reality. This is not the individual who moves quickly from one morsel to the next and cultivates the artificiality of the taster, but the one whose devotion to a form grows profounder as he desires to understand the capacity of others to create different forms and devotions.

We need more than a vision of hope to comprehend a universe that is growing, that develops from within and is moved forward by a divinity that draws it toward himself. Teilhard mentioned that he wondered whether he needed "to go beyond that vision of hope in order to find a basis for a moral attitude to life, and to justify and purify that life. And yet, once again, as a result of contemplating the universe with sympathy and admiration, I felt my belief evolving within me, and I realized that the discovery in and around me of a nascent spirit meant nothing at all if that spirit were not immortal... The universe, *as a whole,* cannot ever be brought to a halt or turned back from a movement which draws it toward a greater degree of freedom and consciousness. This was originally suggested to me by the very nature of the spirit."[6] If this reality is more than a vision of hope, then it is the consequence of science, of paleontological studies, travels, and constant and continuous theoretical

---

[5]Ibid., 28.
[6]Ibid., 38.

investigations of the origins of man and society. Science, like all human reality, is driven by faith, by the power of synthesis, by the constant realization that spirit functions within matter, that the realms of being belong intimately to each other and live from each other. There is a faith that goes beyond particular sacred events and individuals, that is more than history and theology. This is a faith that grows in intensity and breath as it penetrates the growing forces of synthesis that give the universe movement. This faith hovers about the divine that attracts these forces, causing them to grow and unfold, to yield insight into that material-divine movement of evolution that embraces reality.

There is a feeling of joy that comes with the knowledge that my faith has contributed to the architecture of the world. Even though I do not know how this occurs, I do know that it makes a difference if I believe or if I do not. There is a mystery between faith and its consequences, between my conviction and commitment, and my awareness that every being has a particular and peculiar part to play in the sacred evolution of the universe. Teilhard noted that he felt a distinct joy, the "only worthwhile joy as an individual atom in the final establishment of a world: and *ultimately nothing else can mean anything to me.*" Teilhard reminded us that there is a "passion *for being finally and permanently more.*"[7]

These are the feelings that accompany the work of the faithful thinker. The greater he is, the more profoundly conscious he is of the unknown and the mysterious. Like de Tocqueville, Teilhard recognized the impossibility of an encompassing explanation, he knew that "the ultimate currents running deep below the surface of the lives of states and societies will not yield to scientific analysis, but will remain forever mysterious."[8] What we find so attractive and captivating in Teilhard is this openness that he shows to his readers. Each one feels that he is being led into a world where passion and marvels cause him to be hesitant, but also eager to pursue further the journey. At every stage, there is an awakening that defies the effort to find lapidary clarity. Thinking and knowing join feelings and excitements in alliances that are explicit in their vagueness. What is demanded of us by rationality is that expression of thought that is able to describe and clarify an experience that involves not only the mind, but also the body. This experience widens our grasp of faith which engenders itself and is poured forth in ever new channels of life and thought. There is a distinct relationship between vagueness

---

[7]Ibid., 42.

[8]John Clive, *Not By Fact Alone: Essays on the Writing and Reading of History* (Boston: Houghton Mifflin Co., 1989), 36.

and clarity. Here we turn to the artist, to Monet and the facades of the Rouen cathedrals.

With profound insight and sensitivity, Teilhard recognized a movement of reality that others had known but had never structured into what the poet and admirer of Teilhard, Léopold Sédar Senghor, called the *Humanisme de l'Universel* (humanism of the universal). This was a humanism that revealed how necessary it was for man to look also to the heavens for the source of his food. This humanism was subtly and enchantingly described to us in a tale of Franz Kafka, "Investigations of a Dog." There, the investigations of man's foods depended not only on the scratchings of the earth, and its laws, but the fallings from the heavens. "The main part of the food," Kafka noted, "that is discovered on the ground in such cases comes from above." Reception and comprehension joined together in making man aware that the movements from above are linked to those from below, that divisions and separations have little to do with the primordial dependence and enrichment that body and spirit bring to each other. Teilhard's fundamental vision and faith belonged to a fidelity, to a world that "does not hold together 'only from below,' but 'from above.'"[9] This is the primordial intuition that lies at the heart of every great metaphysical vision and reveals the powers of those whose longings for the above are joined with those who yearn to seek them to the world. The movement is circular, a bringing forth from above, animated by the reality which is below, the primordial source and dwelling for what comes upon it from above. Here lies the mystery of being, the marvels of the earthly-heavenly intercourse.

The circular movement is only a preparation for one which opens to us the attracting powers of the divine evaluation, the knowledge and realization that God draws everything toward himself and that it is this moving power that brings from every being and every species the potentialities that lie within it. The fact is that the work of the spirit has only just begun, and that our awareness of the dependence of matter upon spirit, and of spirit upon matter, makes it possible for us to find the nature of our spiritual and moral task. We are aware of the task of the spirit. We refuse to turn from the world and seek sanctuary in isolation and privacy. We turn more fully and courageously toward the earth and find in it the task of the spirit, the meaning of the divine spirit that man knows to be efficacious and purposeful in its dwellings in the world.

Teilhard spoke of the life ahead of us, of a personal universe in which the life of every man and group had a purpose. This universal humanism made it possible for all men to comprehend their lives as

---

[9]*How I Believe*, 45.

fostering and structuring a divine universe which is evolving toward God with an ever-deeper sense of his majesty and sacredness.

Each culture is unique. We are not speaking of a whole into which all the parts melt into the whole and are lost. This would be a false picture of that holy evolution we value so highly, and it would contradict the whole vision of development and change that belongs to every living and organic being which moves toward self-realization and mutual dependency. What is occurring is the movement toward personality in totality. In the depths of the personal, we explore the hints of the universal, the movement of belonging that lives in the personal.

We often find in great men a willingness to speak in the first person, to reveal the experiences of the *I*, the reality that accompanies all that we think and do. We see in the *I* the story of the spiritual journey that each man attempts to undertake and undergo as he reaches out to what he believes is most subjective in him. He discovers what he calls the depths of subjectivity in the most objective experience that he is capable of achieving. The *I* which strives for objectivity longs for the unveiling of a truth that is inseparable from what is most precious and sacred in man, the truth of man's spiritual uniqueness, that is, his subjectivity. Each man and community seeks to discover this truth through history. Teilhard stated this with a sense of fidelity to self and world: "My life's work, it is true, is in some way represented by that part of me which passes into all my fellows; but it is much more fully represented by what I succeed in producing deep within myself, that is incommunicable and *unique*. My personality, that is, the particular center of perception and love that my life consists in developing – it is that which is my real life."[10]

Here, personal consciousness relates to "cosmic consciousness." What is discovered in the human soul is found in the universe whose life is the personal living form of the infinite forms that comprise it. There is a personal center that draws the universe to itself in all its varied manifestations. We could speak of a love that joins the parts to the whole and the whole to its parts. We use these words as symbols and images, but they reveal the life of living beings yearning for their purpose, their place in the universe, and their responsibility for it. We think of the emerging spirit which matter seeks to embody and retake as the child that was lost and has returned. Matter knows spirit and the spirit needs to overcome the evil of separation and dismemberment that rips asunder the primordial unity to which everything belonged. If we think of this "cosmic consciousness" in political and moral terms, we suddenly become aware of the idea that each people reveals in a distinct and particular way different sources and attitudes of the universal humanism

---

[10]Ibid., 52.

of which the poet Senghor spoke. There are no peoples that do not make a cultural contribution to mankind through custom, workmanship, science, or literature. We don't equalize their being, we attempt to see it within a geographical, sociological, and historical framework. We see sparks of divinity.

We explore the nature of religious awareness. If we believe that it is the primordial relationship between man and the world, then it is a relationship that doesn't belong to individuality, but to community. It is a collective experience in which the individual discovers the quality of the self. "To my mind," Teilhard said, "the religious phenomenon, taken as a whole, is simply the reaction to the Universe as such, of collective consciousness and human action in the process of development. Nothing is more mistaken than the view that religion is a primitive and transitory stage through which mankind passed in its infancy. The more man becomes man, the more will it be necessary for him to be able to, and to know how to, worship. The religious phenomenon is only one of the aspects of 'hominization,' and, as such it represents an irreversible cosmic attitude."[11]

These words appear shocking, but are deeply awakening. We realize how we must grow to be men. They play havoc with our traditional attitudes and feelings, making us aware that the forms must yield more to our intuitions than we are often willing to admit. They open to us symbolic possibilities which we must be free to explore with fidelity and truthfulness. We realize that there is a need in the universe, on the earth, and in the spirit to reveal a divinity that makes sacred the "holy evolution" that is taking place in man and the world. Again and again we return to that image of movement from the above and from the below, and we imagine the ladder of Jacob reaching from the earth to the heavens and we guard that sacred movement as the truth of the human experience.

Teilhard often heard the words of Joseph's brothers: "Here comes that dreamer!" If we refuse to allow dreams to be identified with fantasies, if we see them as visions of the future, then the works of Teilhard are pointing us in a direction like those which Joseph showed to his brothers. Teilhard's visions were born not only in dreams, but in the experience of science, in empirical investigations, in writing, traveling, and speaking. He suffered with men of intuition, daring the disdain and jealousy of those who surrounded him. The more he dreamed, the more many of his brothers "hated him even more, for his talk about his dreams." There were those who loved and respected him dearly for his

[11]Ibid., 60-61. See also footnote.

dreams. They embodied in their lives the spirit that mastered their master.

With a touch of melancholic sadness and pain, Teilhard spoke of the clouds that surrounded him. "From so many quarters," he said, "I can hear the summons of this or that divine revelation. To which of these apparently opposed currents am I to surrender myself if the stream is to carry me to the ocean?"[12] We attempt to comprehend the struggle which the mind undergoes in its attempts to see the purpose of its efforts, to clarify the directions it is traveling, to realize the picture it is attempting to detail. Like the artist and the poet, the thinker knows that what he brings forth is in constant development. He knows that it is vagueness that gives him strength, that exaggerated clarity is destructive to thinking. Clarity refuses to allow the imagination to go beyond what it perceives, it confers an unrestrained positivism on what is given. The given becomes the absolute.

The vision of Teilhard is more than a visionary structure. It is metaphysical drama. We are reminded of the spiritual affinities that created the friendship between the painter Monet and the poet Mallarmé. The latter's enthusiasm for Monet was formed by the mystery and allusions which permeated the artist's work. "To evoke an object little by little in order to reveal a state of mind," Mallarmé told an interviewer in 1891, "or, inversely, to choose an object and to derive from it a state of mind by a series of decipherments – that is, the perfect use of mystery."[13] Teilhard's work is more than a scientific hypothesis; it is a poetry of the universe, a painting of vast suggestive beauty into which the faith and fidelity of the religious find its dwellings and manifestations. The work of Teilhard spreads into a universal philosophy. From varied perspectives, we observe the poetic and artistic accompanying the speculative and hypothetical with vigor and command.

Great thought is born in imagery. Vision and thinking are the partners of creative life, the givers of form, the architects of life. The mystery lies in their relationship and intercourse. The constancy of their work, the pain of their dismemberment, form the wonder of human creativity. They reveal a "world of energies" that is infinite in its possibilities. Religious faith is the commitment and fidelity to the spiritualization of the universe, to the upward and downward movement that form the sacred ladder that brings spirit to matter and matter to spirit. Believing in this intensity of movement, in the ever-enhancing dimensions of the universe, is the religious faith that makes

---

[12]Ibid., 62.

[13]Paul Hayes Tucker, *Monet in the 90's* (New York: Yale University Press, 1989), 93.

the divine the consciousness of all reality. Teilhard stated that "faith in the unity of the world, faith in the existence and faith in the immortality of the spirit which is born from the synthesis of the world – these three faiths, summed up in the worship of a personal and personalizing center of universal convergence – these, let me say once more, are the terms of that creed."[14]

We are aware that there are dangers that threaten our religious life, those that come from without and those that come from within. We cannot think of a more debilitating spiritual life than that which proceeds from either an exclusive immersion in external existence, in the everyday habits of societal and familial events, or from a yearning to escape from existence and hide in the fantasies of a disembodied spirit. The imprisonment of the spirit in either life is destructive of the beautiful and the sublime which dwell in the mutuality of world and spirit. Imagine the remark of Paul Valéry: "We are shut up *outside* ourselves." Wherever we turn, we find that the radical revolution in human thought is the liberation from the fixed and definitional in every field of human activity. But it is the religious field more than any other that showed us the way. It showed us the way to the future, to the infinite task of the spirit, the unity of world and divinity.

The image of a "universal cosmic center" becomes the form which men of faith and fidelity can carry in them. They need be neither Christian, Hindu, Jew, Moslem, nor Buddhist; they need only to have been nourished by the spirit and the power of the imagination. The spirit can be spoken of as an evolutionary event, the event that enhances and deepens the human presence of the divine into a reality that is expanding in the self and the universe, that attracts everything toward that personal center from which everything has emerged. In a short work "The God of Evolution" (1953), Teilhard spoke of this phenomenon that infused and gave passion to his work: the event "evolution." He stated: "I am becoming more and more convinced that at the fundamental root of the multiple currents and conflicts it is proper to put the gradual awakening of our generation to the consciousness of a movement of enhancement and cosmic organicism (organicité). The latter leads us, willingly or not, across an unceasing mental edification of a common *Weltanschauung,* toward some 'ultra human,' ahead of us in time."[15]

The image which emerges is like the facade of Monet's Rouen Cathedral. The cathedral is there, but must always be found. There is an emerging clarity that will always remain mysteriously unclear. Allusions

---

[14]*How I Believe*, 64.
[15]"The God of Evolution," in *Christianity and Evolution* (New York: Harcourt Brace Jovanovich, Inc., 1971), 237-43.

will abound in many and multiplying pictures and events; the facade is persistently revealing. The evolutionary movements that fill the universe give us a startling image of the direction that humankind takes in its unceasing attempts to explore the divinity that lives in it and draws all reality toward it.

In Teilhard, the poet, the painter, and the scientist came together, but if we want to discover the laws, the necessary determinations that brought them together, we are at a loss. Like every work of art and religious vision, there are no fixed rules. If we explore the literature of men and women who have been asked to formulate the rules that allow us to see the emerging work of art, we find that no such rules exist unless we are speaking of controlled art and literature. The great thinker is the creator of the world, the symbol, the image, and the living metaphor. The search for truth journeys through the creativity of the arts and the sciences. Although these methods are different, each requires the power of the eye, the intrusion of the illusion, and the sensitivity to mystery. Teilhard's thinking belongs to many perspectives and dimensions. Each is incomplete. The viewer is absorbed in the capacity of thinking to sweep the minds and feelings of others into its architecture, into sacred groves where we find inspiration and love, the guardians of truth and beauty.

The scholars and theologians argue about the religious nature of Teilhard's work, and they will do so for as long as his thought continues to speak to us. Others have found in it inspiration for poetry and politics, for new ways of regarding the universe and being faithful to it. Among them was Léopold Sédar Senghor, poet, politician, essayist, and believer. What he found in Teilhard makes us realize that the greatness of a thinker often denies him his recognition in his own land, but those who come from other lands give him justice. For Senghor, who was president of Senegal for twenty years and who formulated a profound and powerful vision of humankind, Teilhard was a volcanic force that touched and absorbed everything which it approached. What Teilhard could rarely communicate to his own immediate world, he communicated to those who were freer intellectually and aesthetically to comprehend and be inspired by him. Teilhard's thought is like the grainstacks of Monet seen and unseen, wonders of the imagination, marvels of imagery and form. In these wonders and marvels, the divine has always found dwellings.

4

The Gathering of Poets

Senghor dwells in a world of spiritual relationships. For the last sixty-five years, he has studied, written, spoken, and brought forth a literature and poetry which have caused many to admire and honor his work. Senghor, like other poets, artists, scholars, seeks to find the meaning of the act of creation. In this sense, many were influenced by Paul Valéry. In one or another subtle way, Valéry taught decades of literary and artistic men to explore the powers of the imagination, to find in it the essence of man, to find conversation with those for whom creativity has become the substance of life. In other words, it is the Word that has been and will be the sacred union between man and God. The Word is the primordial source of the image, the symbol, the metaphor. Few could escape the force of Gaston Bachelard's *The Psychoanalysis of Fire* (1938), or would want to set aside Henri Bergson's *Essai sur les donneés immédiates de la conscience* (published in English as *Time and Free Will*). Senghor noted that "from the end of the nineteenth century, the pioneers in Western Europe stressed the intuitive reason and the power of the imagination stimulated by sensibility and 'desire.'"[1] The imagination built the bridges from Senegal to France, from the works of the African poets to those who spoke and wrote in French. Senghor was at home in the poetry of Rimbaud, Baudelaire, Valéry, Saint-John Perse, and even more deeply in communication with those who are his contemporaries, Pierre Emmanuel, Jean-Claude Renard, Alain Bosquet. It is not only the associations which are significant, it is what is embraced, what becomes formative, and what stimulates those creative feelings, that enthusiasm and trust which bring forth a work of art or literature. Here we speak of that unexpected and unknown jolt that excites the mind and the emotions and makes us aware of the mystery of the creative experience.

[1]*La Poésie de l'action*, 63.

In his conversations with the Tunisian writer Mohammed Aziza, Senghor spoke of his friendship with his contemporaries. These conversations, covering the last seventy years of his life, became the content of a book: *La Poésie de l'action* (The Poetry of Action). Aziza posed the question: "You have spoken a great deal of the surrealists Peguy and Claudel who exercised a serious influence upon you, but what were your relationships with existentialism?" After stating that he admired Sartre and that the latter was a writer of "genius and generous," Senghor spoke of the friends with whom he had more immediate relationships. "Happily," he said, "I even have friends among the contemporary writers of the generation after Saint-John Perse, like Pierre Emmanuel, Alain Bosquet, Jean-Claude Renard, and let us not forget other Belgians and Canadians. With them, we are preparing to create, we the French writers of the third world, a veritable new literature and consequently, a new civilization of the universal."[2] This idea of the universal accompanied Senghor throughout his life. Although the universal can only be sought in the particular and in the individual, it is the creative light that drives the individual to a reality beyond the self, to the realization that this reality links the individual to the universal. Alive only in the individual, the universal becomes the source of self. Dwelling only in the universal deprives the self of that precious concreteness from which every life begins, and in which each discovers the need to go beyond the self.

Senghor invited the Russian-born Belgian poet Alain Bosquet to visit with him in Dakar. He wanted to speak to him about his idea of a "world capital for poetry." The friends spoke of poetry, of Senghor's *Élégies majeures.* A series of texts came forth from these conversations, exchanges of essays, a poem of Pierre Emmanuel inspired by their conversations. What we have in the essays and poem are reflections on the *Élégies majeures,* serious discussions of the universal dimension of poetry in French, poetry that belongs to five continents and seeks their union, if not their identification. These communications are very significant, as they involve the crossing of boundaries, of traditions, of hopes and visions. The poets must take up this task, their original one. Literature has been the bond between peoples. Again we return to the preciousness of the word, to its powers to give form and create images, to communication through the creative act, to the similarities and parallels that reveal the formative movements that create cultures and their values. We have found the hopes and optimism for the advancement of humankind in the movement of the word. From this perspective, Senghor was the poet-teacher not only for France and for Africa, but for

---

[2]Ibid., 104-5.

men in every land who become conscious of how significant are the relationships between men who comprehend the value of man's creativity. Valéry had discovered in the work of Leonardo da Vinci the marvel of universality, the spirit of investigation, experimentation, and productivity. This spirit brought him to the humanism of the universal. It made him a thinker among men. Senghor knew that we were all students and teachers. We never cease learning, and we never cease teaching. This light of universality forces each of us to step forward and find a way to both give and receive, to create a light within ourselves and show others how it is possible.

The first communication to Senghor from Alain Bosquet was called "Letter to a Poet, Letter to a Continent." He spoke of the poets gathering and the gathering meant communication, learning to listen to the word, to see the image and create form and balance. We might easily set aside such communication between men of spiritual sympathy as unnatural and devised, but it is their communication which serves as the model for others. Bosquet began his letter to Senghor with these words: "For a quarter of a century I read you in the West and there can be no doubt that I harbored the secret hope of becoming, because of you, a little less Western."[3]

Poetry is an expression of how we approach man's place in the universe. We cannot forget that in the West, we have flattered and amused man, catered to his centricity in the world, never forgetting that he was the mediator between the world and the Creator. In his most miserable state, man possessed a dignity and a purposefulness. His life was necessarily precious and we could not refrain from offering him the accolades that belonged to the being whose destiny was somehow linked to divinity. Bosquet thought also of the poetry of the Far East and its contradictory attitude toward man. There, where the precious quality of nature is revered. Man has a subordinate place: placid, tranquil, and artificial. The singular dignity given to him in the West seemed to fade away and man felt that he had been belittled. The poet speaks this language. We feel in his words the reality they create.

Bosquet spoke of the Hindu approach, and thought it might bring a reply to the West. "After Hiroshima," he said, "is it possible for the man thirsting for invisible truth to no longer measure himself by non-being, and by that abstraction which is dormant in each of us to announce our future extinction?" Bosquet further remarked that with Senghor's poems, he made his apprenticeship with Negritude. "I read you as we read Claudel, Cendrars, or Saint-John Perse with an eloquence that is all

[3]"Lettre à un poète, lettre à un continent" in *Oeuvre poétique* (Paris: Editions du Seuil, 1990), 360.

fraternity."[4] This fraternity marks a profound characteristic of Senghor's work. In it lies that rare and precious openness and awareness to new forms and perspectives, new inspirations and sounds, colors and rhythms. The poet's sensitivity to these qualities of man's nature and capacities incline him to what is distinct, different, and similar among men. The poet seeks to give it form, to find the words and then the form that belongs to the words that give shape to thinking. Senghor has that unique sensitivity of expression that joins the powers of the imagination to those of reason. In him, the word is more than the arbitrary tool of the poet. It is the sacred instrument that seeks to reveal the divine Word which lies in every cultural form. The word is the revelatory way that forces the poet to overcome and subordinate the peculiarity of the self. The self searches for the universal, the fraternity of which Bosquet spoke.

Bosquet told Senghor about the impressions which his poems made upon him. He spoke to him of the quality of his poetic verses and what they revealed about the poet. "You grew firm," Bosquet wrote, "by the vehemence of your discourse, although perhaps unknown to you, since a poet owes it to himself to know his marvels and to allow them, at times, to lift him to their level by a levitation which is hardly explicable to him. You forced me, and this was fascinating, to disembody myself a little, to incarnate myself into what you are. This type of transubstantiation between poets does not necessitate a religious ritual. The lucid rite of poetry suffices."[5]

We hold this word transubstantiation with sacred lips; it belongs to the depths of communication and is identifiable with it. Where we speak of one reality, we gather in the other. Yet it is difficult to realize how deeply men relate to others spiritually, how the word, the idea, can move from one to the other, how it can effect a change, form an incarnation, transform the substance and create a new existence. This is our journey to the act of creativity, to that sudden light that changes the quality of the substance, changes the individual and brings forth an unexpected reality. The word transubstantiation has been totally appropriated by the religious and we find it difficult even to think of it as a poetic rite. Yet its imagery and symbolic powers are so great that it must not be allowed to be exclusively thought of religiously. There is a need to cultivate this quality of passage from substance to substance in such a way that there is a change, a miraculous change, a mystery that fascinates and creates the human soul. In this respect, this marvel and wonder heightens and broadens the soul. We speak of a sensitivity that is more and more

---

[4]Ibid., 360.
[5]Ibid.

perceptive to what it touches or sees, feels or hears, that is not mechanical or imitative, but transforming and transfigurative.

Bosquet noted that Senghor had invited him to Dakar three months earlier. "Something quite rare," he remarked, "happened between us without you ceasing to be the first citizen of your country, nor that I had to remove my tie as a man who was too civilized, totally imbued, at the same time, with your colossal fragility. Did we speak too much? Did we exchange proposals that were too explicit? I believe that seeing you on your soil among your compatriots, suddenly suggested to me a diapason between your word and your daily gestures, not only between men but also, if it is possible, between trees and birds. The voice and the show of words in good Western speech, I have always separated them a little from the body which gives them birth. The spirit is finally detached, both from the cranium and the earth which served it both as cradler and grave. There, along the Cape Verde, the reconciliation took place miraculously."[6] Senghor emerged as the diapason, a distinguished image that reveals a man capable of infusing into the things about him a sense of empathy that is rare and precious. If humankind is progressing, then it is the development of this capacity that is required, and it is the poet who shows the way.

The image of the diapason reveals one of the most characteristic qualities of Senghor's thought. He possessed that rare capacity to be a man of many cultures, not simply to describe them but to comprehend them, to be emotionally and spiritually embraced by them. This is that receptive ability which in antiquity became the mark of the poet and the philosopher. It was not the *I* that drove its tentacles into what was perceived, but that ability of the soul to listen and absorb what was given to it by the "light." This receptivity complemented and sobered man's desire to create the world and fellowman through the self, to finally deify this inner light which was the measure of truth. Senghor maintained this balance between the push toward self-deification and that noble and tranquil receptivity of the soul that listens to nature and the divine, and creates from them.

This communication between Bosquet and Senghor is a vehicle by which Africa begins to live in a poet who had not as yet felt its existence. We think of Africa. We know that it is vaster than its poetry, vaster than even the reality of Negritude, and yet we can speak of Africa coming through the poems of the poet, finding in him the wonders of expression, allowing him through rhythm, sound, and word to give us something that will speak to us continually. He does for us what the painter Monet does in his *Gardens of Giverny*, *The Cathedral Doors of Rouen*, or *The*

---

[6]Ibid., 360-61.

Grainstacks. Poems communicate wondrous ideas, feelings, and forms. In the words of the poet, there is a mystery and a marvel that defies our analysis, plays havoc with our analytic reason, with our need for definition and blinding clarity. Bosquet said to Senghor that "all of Africa, this fourth continent of poetry, comes to me in its singularity, in your poems. We grasp the world differently although the poems already, for centuries, belong to our planetary sensibility, and that this acclimatization of African poetry has taken place in French proves that nothing that is essential can be alienated. You have honored us by helping us to understand Africa and you in our language. This letter is practically useless if it were to thank you: we need only 'the telephoning of the heart.'"[7]

These last words of Bosquet, "the telephoning of the heart," is another image that allows us to see the unique place of Senghor in a world struggling to communicate the various cultures that have developed on its surface. Bosquet spoke of the poetry that comes from the West, India and the Far East, that is now joined by that coming from Africa. How, we ask, does man embrace such a world of forms? How does he find the spiritual capacity that would make it possible for him to imbibe the aromas that are born on the different continents? It demands much of his time to learn and become sensitive to the culture of his own language. It would seem that we ask too much of man. He is not a world traveler like Bosquet or Teilhard, he doesn't naturally have a world, not to mention a planetary, vision. Man, like the animals, seeks shelter in the realms of the spirit and of matter. He builds places of rest and comfort. He seeks what is habitual and traditional. He rests comfortably with the traditions he has inherited from family, society, and religion. The capacity to bridge worlds is rare indeed. We look upon it with hope and wonder; it is similar to the power of the Idea. We know that it is there, that it has been enunciated through the ages. We hear the words of the biblical Prophets. We speculate about the naiveness of the prophetic vision. We wonder why men can dream the ideal if by the real we mean the inscrutable events that shape our biological lives. Nothing is more real than conflict, pain, death, and incurable illnesses. Yet the Idea remains an unextinguishable power. It has more reality than a gadfly; it infuses our existence and drives us toward ever-new forms and images.

The poet Jean-Claude Renard began his letter to Senghor by quoting him: "I, the Master-of-language, My task is to awaken my people to future splendors / My joy is to create images of nourishment, rhythmic lights from the world."[8] With these lines Renard believed Senghor voiced

---

[7]Ibid., 362.
[8]"Ma Négritude est truelle à la main," in *Oeuvre poétique*, 363.

the demon of poetry. He conformed his language both to his place among his people and to the world which they embraced. He spoke as the poet-philosopher; the word of his people was formed in his mind and on his lips. He sent forth their word to a listening humankind anxious to know of another segment of the family that now voices its longings and vision of the universe, that wants that fraternity that makes the human community.

Jean-Claude spoke of Senghor's capacity to make poetry speak the voice of his situation. "The *voice* of a great poet," Renard noted, "knows how to create a language exactly in conformity to his situation, as a French-speaking African embodying several cultures, a language capable of being primordial and unique, unifying all the diverse currents which nourish it. Here word, song, and music become identical and where the analogous image emerges 'under the effect of the rhythm,' 'time and space creating the favorable distance, even the meter and verse of the organ.'"[9] Senghor's poetry is not a vague expression of the humanism of the universal. It speaks universally as it reflects the language of his people. In its most intimate and distinct sounds and rhythms, it embraces the encompassing universalism. Its individuality makes it possible to appreciate similar voices in other peoples. Only the individual who has read or prayed with the Psalms is attuned to that love of God to whom others pray with their poetry. Touched by the longing for divinity, the poet creates with love the wings that bear him to it.

Renard ennobled Senghor with the title of "Sayer-of-Very-Hidden-Things," who "pursues the pureness of his passion, works in quest of the 'fresh milk of truth,' in quest of the 'Renaissance of Meaning and of the Spirit,' of the 'revelation of Beauty.'"[10] Renard strings together these images from Senghor's poetry to construct pictures of the poet's adventure. First we are told that he reveals hidden things, that he harbors truths that are not given to the ordinary man, that he has been given the art of language to reveal them to his fellowmen. In every great figure, there lies a marvel, a magic, which make others wonder at the sublimity of the creative act and its product. This is accompanied by a truth, or the search for it, which other men do not intend to undertake even if they, at one time, harbored the possibility of it. True to the poetic nature is the search for a rebirth of meaning and a strengthening of the spirit. Driven by the demon of love, both the philosopher and the poet live with the reality of the Idea. The poet comprehends the meaning of the jolt. He works through transformation and transmutation. What is concrete and immovable, determined and unchangeable, is suddenly

[9]Ibid.
[10]Ibid., 364.

brought to a new reality in and through metamorphosis. In this radical change truth is born. Kafka revealed this in his famous story "Metamorphosis." The truth of Gregor Samsa is revealed in the first sentence of the story: "As Gregor Samsa awoke one morning from uneasy dreams he found himself transformed in his bed into a gigantic insect." This was the truth of Gregor Samsa which only the metamorphosis revealed. Senghor knew that what appeared in Africa had a profound reality which the poet alone could transfigure and transform. The truth lay in his demon. The demon never left him, but drove him from vision to vision, from dream to dream.

Poetry was for Senghor an act of statesmanship. It was his vehicle of communication even though he was a member of government, a head of state, and a world diplomat. If his scholarly work lay in abeyance, the poet who spoke of "very hidden things" continued to speak to the world through essays, speeches, and conference lectures. Renard properly remarked that for Senghor, "the poetic act is also a *way of life and a making of life.* 'For you, nothing but this poem against death.' The poet, like his word, is the 'sign of recognition' between beings and things. He wants to be the man of 'faithful blood who needs fidelity.' I know that he is and remains, above all else, an African who refuses to allow his blood to become meaningless 'like the assimilated and the civilized.' Even his Christian faith was opposed to that of his fathers'."[11]

Senghor's way of life was created in poetry, but this term indicates that he was a maker, an active doer in the world of ideas, a man of faith who lived from fidelity. He required it from others. For many, he was the "knight of faith." He left one land to go to another, to bring to both a new message of hope and optimism. The messenger knows he bears a truth which the world is not prepared to hear, neither his own people, nor the others. In every generation there are a few men who bear a message for others, but their loneliness and despair test their will, and they seek the strength to pursue with their demon the hidden God whose message is untranslatable, but whose presence is felt in the formation of words and forms.

Renard looked upon Senghor as the "ambassador of the black people," but he was also a man deeply dedicated to the idea of humankind. He spoke to all peoples; he sang of his love for the earth from which all peoples emerged and for which they bear responsibility. He called upon men to find pride in their contributions to each other, to seek to extend them. It is in human cooperation that we discover the precious words that are given in the message that Senghor has for humankind: the humanism of the universal.

---

[11]Ibid., 365.

Pierre Emmanuel sent his remarks to Senghor in a poem entitled "A Léopold Sédar Senghor." We quote a few lines which announce the message:

Qui est notre par toi
Toi l'Africain
Héritier par droit de naissance
d'Empires de l'âme qui nous sont inconnus,
Comme son amant se choisit son aimée
- Et c'est aussi adopter une mére –
Tu est devenu le fils et l'epoux
D'une autre ténèbre d'une autre lumiére
Grecque et numide Mediterranée

What can ours be for you
You the African
By birthright inheritor of spiritual
realms unknown to us
Like the lover choosing the beloved
It is also adopting a mother
You have become the son and the husband
From a darkness, from a light
Greek and Numidian Mediterranean.[12]

Again and again, we hear this call made to Senghor, the bearer of the mysterious voice of the African continent. Emmanuel turns to him to hear the continent speak. But he is not only the poet of Africa, he speaks also from the civilizations of the Mediterranean; he speaks from Africa to the Occident and from the Occident to Africa. He reveals the possibility of surpassing cultural frontiers, a path to that rare openness of which Teilhard had spoken. We touch upon this distinct quality when we read Emmanuel's poem. We hear the sounds of the words, envision the images, and listen to the beauty of the spiritual conversation that flows from poet to poet. We imagine the world they attempt to construct, the need they feel to reveal their fidelity to the earth and to each other. Poetry draws its themes from the great spiritual forces that emerge in man and his work. These forces call to the poet to give sound and rhythm to what comes forth and needs to be spoken. Is poetry, we ask, only in the service of its greatest and encompassing spirits? We leave the answer open. We are inclined to say yes.

Poets have reminded us to avoid too close of a relationship between poetry and politics, and the latter can be a true danger. Poets have sadly eulogized dictators and they have fought political battles, but the disturbances of the poet or the writer cannot lessen our need for the words, for the beauty and goodness of the universal message and the

---

[12]"A Léopold Sédar Senghor," in *Oeuvre poétique,* 367.

poetic forms which it should take. When this message is beyond the immediate needs of men, when it flows from the universality of the divine, it can be nothing other than incantations and rhapsodic prayers which have always revealed the inspiration of the poetic muse.

In response to Alain Bosquet, Pierre Emmanuel, and Jean-Claude Renard, Senghor wrote a long letter entitled "Letter to Three Poets of the Hexagon," which began with the remark that he wanted to speak not simply as a black, but as a French writer, and that it was more important to speak of what brings us together, France and Africa, than what separates us. He also wanted to make it clear that each man comes from a mixed heritage and that the future belonged to this integration of peoples, *"l'avenir est au métissage."* No culture is so pure that it bears no comparison with another, no culture's forms are so unique that they can be understood only from a single perspective. Rather, we become more and more aware of the mystical and symbolic nature of a culture, how it forms its relationships between man and God, between man and the earth. In these relationships, we are exposed to architecture, ritual, initiations, incantations, music, and poetry. Senghor reminded us that "we cannot leave the Negro-African mystique without recalling that its symbolism is not only the object of knowledge, but of practice not only through ritual ceremonies, with their words, poems, chants, gestures, and masked dancers, but above all, by the life of the iniates who live by their symbolism, to be sure, each in his spirit, and even more in his body and soul, transforming himself, 'converting' himself into a god, more exactly into God."[13] What we bear witness to is the inseparability of body and soul, that union that makes it possible for truth to find its dwelling. For the poet, this truth is his poems, the embodiments of his life, of the spirit which is identifiable with it and which is in persistent search of the home he calls the union of body and soul.

Senghor knows that the poet does not escape his demon. Speaking to his colleagues, Senghor said that "the fact [is] that for each of us poetry is in our life, not the profession [*métier*], but the major activity, the life of our life, without which the latter would not be life."[14] In the introduction to his study of Alain Bosquet, in the series *Poets of Today*, Pierre Emmanuel confessed: "My true domain is poetry, poetry and the reflection on it." We read these words with satisfaction and understanding, but we find it difficult to penetrate the subtle depths of this reality for those who live the poetic life, and the poetry of the human reality. We are not dealing with academics, but with men who know that they are expressing the voice of their cultures, the voice of men who seek

[13]"Lettre à trois poètes de l'hexagone," in *Oeuvre poétique*, 374.
[14]Ibid., 377.

freedom and believe in the future. If we think for a moment of the Psalms, we realize the power of these prayers – the voices that attempt to awaken this power in other men, to reveal their need for a relationship with God, their desire to sing and chant their most delicate and forceful feelings – and we begin to understand the poetry of Senghor. Senghor's view of the poet places the latter in the center of civilization. Along with men of science and literature, the poet is the carrier of a divine message. He reveals the infinite powers of the human spirit. He is capable of giving it form and structure. In him, the word incarnates the universality of man's deepest emotions, the "light of silence."

Senghor stresses this identification of poetry and life. He quotes from Jean-Claude Renard's *Incantations des eaux* (Incantations of the Waters). Renard spoke of poetry when he wrote: "It is probable that the poet can only speak of one thing, of the unique mystery which lives in his caverns and labyrinths. This mystery possesses, fascinates, and overwhelms him, but it finally guides him... to the center of this silence where the single word of importance begins, the one which justifies man."[15] However we attempt to grasp this distinguished role of the poet, we arrive at the fact that we are involved in a vision of the world, and it is this vision that makes it possible to deal with the politics of everyday life. Perhaps we say too much when we affirm that the poet belongs to political life. We know that his belief in human freedom and in the act of creativity makes him a being whose activity is ultimately in contradiction to every manner and mode of totalitarianism.

We could speak of a unique mystery as the "vital force" which heralds the birth of the creative act. Senghor spoke of Bosquet's commentary on Emmanuel's *Reflexions préliminaires* (Preliminary Reflections) and referred to his attempt to comprehend the poet's inspiration as *élan vital.* "Nothing," Senghor noted, "seems to me more just, because in black Africa the reality that underlies all apparent realities, is the *Force vitale.* Emmanuel spoke of this reality in his studies on poetry... and he designated it by such expressions as 'calling in the night,' 'the messenger is preceded by his cry,' 'the silent visitation of the Other.' He embraces these metaphors in these words: that – this reality which speaks in the night, which prefers the nocturnal silence – comes to you from the depths of your self, and before appearing reveals its voice."[16]

Whether we speak of *élan vital, force vitale,* or *élan créateur,* we speak of the Muses which animate the soul, which give life purpose and imagery. Senghor comes to us as a child of the Muses, and the metaphors

[15] Ibid.
[16] Ibid., 385.

we use to grasp his vision remain paths without definitions, clarifications without finality, comprehension without a system of concepts. The fact that Senghor remains beyond the clarity of the fixed form creates his beauty. He infuses excitement in those who read him, and nobility in those who study him. He spoke often of "the sacred character of the poetic word" because he had a sense of the sacred. He accepted its appearance in nature, in the finitude of things that are about us. He knew it to be the primordial source of life. He felt its presence as Socrates did when he spoke to Diotima of Mantinea, the midwife of beauty, to Homer who honored the Muses. The world is not an arbitrary architecture. Forces of creativity live within it. They await the liberation which depends upon man's work. We think of the "divine sparks" hidden in the skills that long for their unfolding. Wherever we touch the poetic, we are brought into a world of images and symbols, myths and metaphors that fill our imagination and drive us to ever-new levels of understanding. We know that the mysteries of the creative élan lay not only within us, but beyond us. They give us messages. We hear their voices, but they deny us, with cleverness, the fullness of their reality. They refuse us the demon of self-deification.

Senghor mentioned with admiration the work of the Sengalese thinker Alassane Ndaw. Ndaw's work carried the title *La Pensée africaine: Recherches sur les fondaments de la pensée négro-africaine* (1983), (African Thought Studies: Concerning the Foundations of Negro-African Thought). The work so impressed Senghor that he recommended it to his friends. He was particularly impressed with Ndaw's discussion of African thought and mysticism. He quoted Ndaw's statement that "the fundamental function of the word is to hide. The hiding is not an end in itself and contains, implies, the fact of revealing. The word thus establishes the initiation into necessity."[17] We touch in the movement from hiding to revealing not only the work of the poet, but of the creator in all fields of human endeavor. There is no identification between what is signified and our capacity to grasp and comprehend it. There is a gap. At times it is profound and we need the powers of imagery, myth, and metaphor to attempt to relate the object to the subject. Often, the object is greater than the thinking subject, but at times, the thinking subject can be greater than its object. We fit the objects into our thinking. We realize that the object and the subject belong to each peripherally. We use analogies to make some sense of the relationships. This failure to find the balance between thinking and the object is significant. Into the gap rushes man's creative capacities, not knowing, and perhaps never happily achieving the identification of subject and object. Man discovers

[17]Ibid., 390.

in this gap the nature of his humanity. Having been denied the knowledge of absolutes, the tree of good and evil, his merciful God allowed him to develop his power of judgment. Man, partly free from the cyclical powers of natural necessity, develops a poetic world of myths which do not hinder the advancement of his knowledge, but reveal its limitations and incompleteness.

In conclusion, Senghor spoke of his seven elegies, *Elegies Majeuris,* dedicated to his wife Colette, to Claude Pompidou, to Habib Bourguiba, and to Martin Luther King, Jr. "I hope," he said, "to convince the reader who will have read the *Major Elegies* after having finished this letter. If I placed this collection, like those which preceded it, in its context – French but yet worldly, with the accent on black Africa – it was to hand them over to the truth of the twentieth century: to the civilization of the universal."[18] We sing together the songs of our visions and hopes. They bind us together as men and poets, searching for what is human and humane in the hearts of men. We sing of death and suffering, of the unexpected human loss, of destiny and reconciliation, of the need to speak with God, to take him into ourselves, to question the portion of life he gives and takes from us. "Of what do we sing," Senghor asks, "if not of the essential substances, the beings who hold up sensible appearances. They possess this supreme virtue of being transmuted, transcending their being and achieving the *plus-être,* in becoming fully human? What do we sing if not the poetic word, the fecund word, which transforms, by converting us, we the poets, into divine beings?"[19]

We are again returned to the word that hides and reveals, that transforms and transfigures, that brings about the metamorphosis and the mystery of being. Senghor knows that the word has been spoken over the forces of the earth and the poet listens and hears the word when it is revealed. What he hears is an unveiling of the hidden, glimmers of the light of its silence. With the word, man is freed of the doctrinaire and the ideological. The word has a magic power that never allows it to be identified with a given object where it dies in the monotony of repetition. In his *Elegies,* Senghor sang of the human destiny, songs men hear as they listen to the traditions of their cultures, as they listen to voices of other men singing of their faith and the sadness of their fate.

With concluding words, Senghor spoke of a hope that accompanied his life, that grew in depth as he grew in understanding and faith. "I speak," he declared, "of a *poïëtique* word which creates a new economic order – we must eat to be sure – like a new world cultural order. I speak of a word as a new vision of the universe and, at the same time, a pan-

[18]Ibid., 407.
[19]Ibid.

human creation. I speak for the last time of the *fecund Word*, as a fruit of different civilizations created by all the nations together on the face of planet earth."[20] In our attempt to comprehend these words, we discover that they are not like those of experimental science, they are not quantitative terms which measure and weigh. They are qualitative terms which hide and reveal, which for some are vague, for others stimuli, incitements for the imagination. We approach these words from perspectives which either allow us to appreciate them or force us to turn away with skepticism and disbelief. What we know is that behind the words lives a man who is statesman and poet, who acted and judged, who told the world that he believed in human dignity and freedom. In speaking of these things with that rare power of imagery, he gives his form of expression eternal beauty. He speaks to us. His voice is heard in all the lands. He speaks of the humanism of the universal, of the mixture of peoples. He holds before us a dream, telling us that we have a right and obligation to dream. We need to know that men grow spiritually strong when they learn from their fellowmen, when they are open to them, and comprehend the humanism of fraternity.

---

[20]Ibid., 408.

5

Poetic Companions: Claudel and Senghor

In 1928, a lonely, young Senegalese man arrived in Paris, the center of European civilization. It was the city of Gide, Bergson, Valéry, Claudel, Colette, the city of ballet, theater, art. To this city came writers and poets from the West Indies, from the United States, and Africa, men and women who sought to find a cultural capital, to share their complaints and hopes, to find companionship and fraternity. "Historical essays about black Africa and vivid accounts of racial injustice," Janet Vaillant noted, "were set side by side with discussions of African art, West Indian music, and black American poetry. Contributors ranged from white writers such as Pound, Theodore Dreiser, and William Carlos Williams, to black activist Americans W.E.B. Du Bois and Walter White. Figures important to the Harlem Renaissance, notably Alain Locke, Langston Hughes, Countee Cullen and Sterling Brown, were also represented, as were Africans who would later be active in the movement for independence, such as Nnande Azikiwe and A.A. Ademola."[1]

Senghor had come to the most renowned lycée in France, to Louis-le-Grand founded by the Jesuits in 1563, the school of Molière, Baudelaire, Hugo, Jaurès, Durkheim, Georges Sorel, Marquis de Sade. The tradition was enough to overwhelm an incoming student, one who was a poet, who loved the word, and who would become one of its great masters. A great master arises from others. Senghor sought his teachers not only among those who were at Louis-le-Grand, but in the poets Paul Claudel, Arthur Rimbaud, and Charles Baudelaire. He found in them what is essential to learning: fascination, admiration, inspiration, and wonder. They taught him the power of the imagination, the nature of the creative

[1]*Black, French, and African*, 65.

act, an openness to reality, and that evolutionary process which revealed the mutability of all things.

Senghor remarked in his *Ce que je crois* (What I Believe), that Claudel's poetry was a link between his Senegalese tradition and the poetry he discovered in Rimbaud. In fact, he found that Claudel's work was a way to comprehend his African traditions. In particular, there was a short essay of Claudel entitled "Ma Conversion" (1913) (My Conversion) which particularly moved Senghor. The work is profound in its grasp of the soul's search for transcendence, of the need of every creative being to find a way to overcome the dominance of everyday existence. Every being searches for a meaning, every culture seeks to offer its explanations of man's relationship to the universe and to transcendence. In Claudel, Senghor discovered a parallel to his own conversion into the world of poetry and its universal expression. The idea of conversion speaks not only of radical change, but of constant and persistent changes in the modes of life. These subtle and significant differences in orientation and perspective create new ways of understanding and knowing reality. These are the forceful elements in our continuous transformation of self and circumstances.

Paul Claudel (1868-1955) was a poet, a disciple of Mallarmé, deeply attracted to the volcanic emergence of ideas and forms in the poetry of Rimbaud. But it was the religious experience which he underwent at Notre Dame in Paris on Christmas 1886, that became the light that guided his future work. Nothing which happened subsequently was free of this dominating love and passion for God and his church. It was this power of love that gives reality to all creation. It is the attracting force which conditions the artist in his desire to bring forth new forms and a new spirit from whatever he perceives and seeks to know.

Senghor quoted from "Ma Conversion" words that embodied his own experience of the conversion that would continue throughout his life. He recalled these words of Claudel: "We recall the sad years of the 1880s, the epoch of the full expansion of naturalistic literature. Never did the yoke of matter seem better established. Everyone who had a name in the arts, sciences, and literature, was irreligious.... At eighteen, I believed everything which the majority of cultivated people at the time valued. The forceful idea of the individual and the concrete was hazy to me. I accepted the monistic and mechanistic hypothesis in all its rigor. I believed that everything was subject to law and that this world was an immutable chain of causes and effects which science would clarify perfectly in the immediate future. All this seemed to me deeply sad and frightfully boring.... The first glimmer of truth was given to me through the encounter with the books of a great poet to whom I owe eternal recognition, and who had a predominant part in the formation of my thought. He was Arthur Rimbaud.... The reading of *Illuminations* and, several months later, of *Une Saison en enfer* [A Season in Hell] was a momentous event. For the first time these books forced a crack in my materialist prison and gave me the living and almost physical impression of the supernatural."[2]

We can imagine the impact this text had on Senghor. He chose to cite these words because he knew they spoke of the voyage he was taking as he moved from Senegal to France, and from France to the world, to that planetary vision of Teilhard which would later embrace and mold his life.

Referring to the specific influence of Claudel upon his thought, Senghor remarked: "Paul Claudel, after Rimbaud and more than Rimbaud, influenced me by making me return to the sources of Negritude.... In his poems as in his dramas, Paul Claudel, after Arthur Rimbaud, goes back to the aesthetic of the Negro-African word and to the dynamic multivalence which is spiritual in its images. Because it is this way, we rarely find comparisons, but almost always metaphors, metonymies, and catachreses."[3] We realize from Senghor's remarks how marked is the road from one poet to another. The domination of a perspective, of a spiritual commitment, determines what we find in another poet or writer. We come to every spiritual heritage with a power of receptivity. There were words and expressions in Claudel and Rimbaud that were received by Senghor with joy and satisfaction. He found recognition of the people of Ham, an appreciation of a culture which was dear to his tradition. Tradition was the source of his life. Tradition would always be the foundation of his poetic expression.

Senghor, in 1972, dedicated his contribution at the International Conference of Brangues to "La Parole chez Paul Claudel et chez les Negro-Africains" (The Word in Paul Claudel and in the Negro-Africans). Senghor sought for the bridges which link culture to culture. We would say that his spiritual architecture developed from this constant attempt to forge ways to join peoples to each other, not by identifying these ways, but by showing people how to communicate with each other, and how they might comprehend this communication as the way of that world spirit that draws from cultures their possibilities and distinctions and makes us realize how deeply dependent we are upon each other even with the differences which seem to separate us abysmally.

Senghor at Brangues looked back and he found what had made it possible for him to look forward, to envision a planetary conception of

---

[2]*Ce que je crois: Négritude, Francité et Civilisation de l'Universel* (Paris: Bernard Grasset, 1988), 211.
[3]Ibid., 214.

the universe, to identify his conception of the future with that of Teilhard. Teilhard had courageously formulated his vision and given it bold expression. "In short," Teilhard said, "humanity has reached the biological point where it must either lose all belief in the universe or quite resolutely worship it. This is where we must look for the origin of the present crisis in morality. But it is necessary also for the religions to change themselves in order to meet this new need. The time has passed in which God could simply impose Himself on us from without, as master and owner of the estate. Henceforth, the world will only kneel before the organic center of its evolution. What we are all more or less lacking at this moment is a new definition of holiness."[4] From a perspective so powerful and revolutionary, the world of ideas and relationships would undergo as radical a change as it suffered in the great revolutions at the end of the eighteenth century. Senghor was a poet of this upheaval. He discovered its signs in the world of Rimbaud, Claudel, and the philosopher Henri Bergson, whose *Creative Evolution* (1908) had brought wonder to the American philosopher William James. Senghor's genius lay in his openness to the marvels in literature and poetry which he found in the 1880s. His genius embraced with noble simplicity the inspiration of creative activity. Senghor felt this activity with creative sympathy. It became his flesh and spirit. He lived from the creativity of beauty.

Senghor did not come to Claudel to embrace his every work, to master him in the details and footnotes of a dissertation. He came to Claudel because he found in him links to his own Senegalese tradition. He found in him a poet who excited his own poetical proclivity. Senghor noted that "as a student and teacher, and above all as a poet, I analyzed Claudel's poetry. I attempted to comprehend it, to *assimilate* it by referring myself essentially to the Negro-African *Word* expressed in his poems."[5] There was something more than assimilation and comprehension between Senghor and Claudel. There was a dynamic opening to a world that was no longer closed, that made truth and transcendence interchangeable. Senghor noticed this when he thought about the reasons which brought him close to Claudel. He remarked: "I perceived at the same time that the poet often in his living interpretations was close to Teilhard de Chardin and also to Negro-African thought. Claudel, like the sap which inflates the bud, expands a narrow orthodoxy until it bursts."[6] This was the Claudel of his youth, the poet

---

[4]*Human Energy* (New York: Harcourt Brace Jovanovich, 1969), 110.
[5]"La Parole chez Paul Claudel et chez les Negro-Africains," in *Liberté* (Paris: Editions du Seuil, 1977), 3:348.
[6]Ibid., 350.

who showed him how to heighten and broaden the word, and deepen the spiritual bridge which led from Senegal to France, and then to build an even greater one which would lead toward a new vision of the world. This world order is rooted in a sacred evolutionary process which God, in his holiness, draws forth from humankind. With all the similarities that Senghor drew from the poetry of Claudel, he was ultimately interested in more than appreciations and reflections on Africa in French poets. If a humanism of the universal did not emerge from these spiritual dialogues, we would find these comparisons interesting if only for the moment.

Senghor noted that both Claudel and the Negro-Africans had the same worldview, "*a Weltanschauung* which is essentially an ontology..., a science of being, a coherent order of principles and ideas which explain beyond the nature of things, the structure of the world and the relationships between beings, that is, between the elements of matter and spirit."[7] This is not the architecture of discursive reason, of the intellectualism which Bergson attempted to lay to rest, but the intuition of the poetic, the creation of the poetic, of the poet, a reality that is lived and felt. It was in Claudel's *Art poétique* (Poetic Art) and his *Traité de la co-naissance au monde et de soi-même* (Treatise of Co-Birth in the World from the Self) that Senghor found the insights for a poetical creation that would ultimately lead to a new humanism founded in a metaphysical mutuality which would not only show the dependency of cultures upon each other, but would create a community of communication that would allow antagonistic cultures to find their way to dialogue with those they believe have little to give them. Each culture needs not only to comprehend its ontology, but also the bridges it must build to others. If Claudel or Rimbaud or Bergson was Senghor's way back to Africa, they were ways beyond Africa to the world, to a universality as yet unknown, but only contemplated and believed.

Senghor did not only find comparative ideas in Claudel's work, he also admired his depths of faith. He read *Ma Conversion* intensely and we have cited his words, but the levels of these emotions touched him deeply. The religious emotion develops as the text is read again and again through the years. Claudel, like any great poet-philosopher, is studied throughout a life of exploration and search. In describing his conversion in 1886 at Notre Dame, Claudel said: "I was in the crowd, near the second column at the entrance to the choir, at the right alongside of the sacristy. Then the event occurred which dominated my entire life. In a moment, my heart was touched and *I believed;* I believed with such an adhesive force, with such an upheaval of my whole being, with a

---

[7]Ibid.

conviction that was so powerful, with a certitude that left no place for doubt. Since then, all the books, all reasoning, all the haphazardness of a restless life could not overwhelm my faith and could not touch it. Suddenly I had the torturous feeling of innocence, of the eternal childhood of God, of an unutterable revelation."[8]

We have no similar incident in Senghor's life, but we have the spiritual jolts which opened to him constantly new spiritual perspectives and faith. Faith dominates his work, faith in man and humankind, an optimism and a sense of emerging spiritual energies. Senghor's faith was always near to Teilhard's belief in a sacred evolution. Senghor felt close to those whose faith dominated their vision and drove them from static to dynamic ventures of the human soul. God was not the judge dominating their daily existence. He was the attracting power that drew men from their caves to new ventures into the spiritual community and fraternity. The demon of faith made it possible for Senghor to find in Claudel an early mentor. The fascination of the creative believer, of Claudel, left its indelible mark on Senghor.

If Senghor found the faith of Claudel, at times, rigid, he found at the same time a delicate subtlety of interpretation which opened to him a divine activity. On the surface it would appear as if God is everything and man, the sinner, a miserable and disdained creature. Yet this dualism between the majesty of God and the sinfulness of man may yield to something grandiose. "Do like the Muse," Senghor noted, following Claudel, "and repeat the creation finding work and joy – the aim itself of our life – in this repetition." The lines of Claudel's poem "Les Muses" reveal this truth:

> But like the holy God who created each thing.
> Your joy is in the possession of its name.
> And as he said in silence 'Let it be!'.
> It is thus, full of love.
> You repeat what he has named.[9]

No longer is man's work only the sweat of Cain, but like the holiness of God, his work is noble and sublime. The love of the creation gives man the power to seek in it the divine hand, to realize that it has only just begun to realize its truths, to make us aware of how groundless are its depths and how unfathomable its beauty. Man is not naive or blinded to the evil that lies in him, to the destructive disorder that belongs to nature, but he knows that he bears within him the power to control, if not to dispel, these forces. He knows that even the violence that

---

[8]"Ma Conversion," in *Oeuvres en prose* (Paris: Pléiade, Gallimard, 1965), 1010.
[9]"La Parole chez Paul Claudel," 352.

surrounds him and lives in the reality he seeks to know is part of the spiritual evolution of humanity.

This evolution, this humanism of the universal is the continuous release of energies that lie in matter. In fact, Senghor tells us that in Bantou "being is what possess force," that *"being Is force."* This force is love, the solidarity among men, the intimate love of man and woman, the knowledge that in every man there is a woman and in every woman a man. From the spiritual community of the couple emerges the "Communion of Saints." Claudel found in this image the sublime songs of his poetry; it was an image that moved him deeply. It was the image of the emotional bonds that linked humankind and gave every man and culture a place in the divine harmony, in the music that rose from the divine creation. Senghor remembered that when he read some of Claudel's poems, they evoked in him a sadness about the bitterness of life, but then there was always the "flame of spirituality" and a hope, that constant interplay of pain and joy that weaves the harmony of human life. When man has forsaken his search for happiness, a search that has no purpose and ends in weakness and surrender, he discovers the human interplay of opposites that give his life harmony and music. Claudel remarked in his "Treatise of Co-Birth" that "in this bitter mortal life, the most poignant delicacies revealed to our nature are those which accompany the creation of soul through two bodies. They are only the humble image of this meaningful embrace in which the soul, learning its name, and the intention which it satisfies, will come forth to liberate itself, inhaling and exhaling in turn."[10] There is a rhythm in the image that deeply attracted Senghor. The choices he makes from Claudel's work reflect the intoxication of the music of biblical harmonies that ceaselessly permeated Claudel's poetry.

The dependence of reality upon realities comes forth again and again in both Claudel and Senghor. In Claudel's "L'Esprit et l'eau" (The Spirit and the Water), we hear words of dialogue which allow us to feel the depths of the divine-human intercourse:

> You are there and I am there
> And you do not let me pass and I also do not let you pass
> And you are my end, and I also am your end."

God and man are together in the world. They call to each other. Samuel heard the voice of God three times and to each call he said: "Here I am, you called me." The imagery of the voice calling makes us aware that we are not alone. We belong to a universe in which the calling of the divine is the drawing power that reveals to us both our loneliness and

---

[10]Ibid., 357.

dependence. We are being born with each other. We form a harmony and a disharmony; we hear the voice like Samuel did and we maintain our deafness. This "being born with" is a symbol of the relationship of things to each other. "Because we are with the plants, animals, minerals, all the phenomena of nature," Senghor reminds us, "we can know them at the frontier of our being, by our movement at the same time as by theirs. In other terms, by our senses. Our senses because we have been created in the divine image. We are a double microcosm of God and of the world. We are thus constructed as an active *intelligence* capable of movement, spiritual matter, an operative form, taking the form of beings who are exterior to us, simple appearances, and making them realities."[11]

Man stands within the creation of sensible being, among the plants and animals. He is more than intellect, more than the creator of concepts in which he seeks to explain himself and the world about, he is a being who has found mutability in all things, who has set aside absolutes and discovered the incompleteness of the universe, who knows truth only in change and evolution, who realizes that in the imagery of Bergson and Teilhard we revolutionized our concept of the universe and created a vision of the expanding and growing universe. Claudel remarked that "the intelligence perfects things, reduces them to the spirit, to the movement by which they reveal, by fleeing, the movement at its origin and end, by which the living being forms in his body proportion and idea. It is the image of things comprehending and consummating the intelligible host in which they are consummated."[12] Here we find the individual creating, through the union of spirit and body, the sacredness of creation. He is the being who can bless the creation, bring forth from the appearances which form his perceptions the spiritual source from which they emerge. Through the Benediction, the separation of the so-called division of noumena and phenomena disappears. What is impossible for the intellect to conceive is brought about in the act of a consecrating faith which expands through the universe and makes us aware that we bear within ourselves the capacity to restore the original unity between thinking and its object. The voice of God, which Samuel heard, and Eli didn't, is the voice that will be continually heard by men as they become more aware of how significant it is to lessen the distance between man's hopes and God's will.

If we seek to comprehend Senghor, and the Negro-African concept of reality, we find that truth lies in the acceptance of sensuality as the fundamental link between man and his world. Sensuality is a feeling for the concreteness of the natural form, an ability to grasp it through touch,

[11]Ibid., 360-61.
[12]Ibid., 361.

smell, sound, taste, and sight. We, on the other hand, have through an exaggerated concept of the mind, disembodied our being, giving to the mind a majesty which we deny to the senses. This disembodiment of the human reality has cut us off from those qualities of life which form our senses, and from an appreciation for subtle feelings and emotions. Senghor stated that "sensuality yes, but not eroticism, emerges from the separation of body and mind, intelligence and sentiment. Sensuality is the gift by which we seize the sensible qualities of the external world, through all the senses whose organizing movements Claudel well described. Grasping and living them in the forms, colors, movements of the animals, the plants, the minerals, natural phenomena in their sounds and rhythms, their juices, flavors, and tastes, even in their textures and in their fabrics. For the Negro-Africans, rooted as they are in the concrete, sensuality is as a word, a life beyond the pleasure of the senses, an identification with the other, either as person or object, in the joy of union: of communion...a spiritual phenomenon."[13]

With these words, Senghor allows us to enter the world of rhythms and movements that permeate his poetry, his imaging of the world. Here lives that harmony of relationships which man continually and persistently seeks to comprehend but not dominate, to find in them the knowledge which pulsates with life and meaning. In these relationships, we discover the oneness of creation, its movements toward higher unities, and the divine attraction that draws all reality toward itself, bringing out of each the essence that lies in it. This is what Teilhard called the "fall forward." Senghor, in every interpretation he makes, reminds us that it is Teilhard whose depth of intuition gives us the most comprehensive and sublime vision of the universe. Senghor quoted Teilhard with approval when the latter stated that "stage by stage, it [the fall forward] must go on till the end of the world. And finally, it is the total center itself, much more than the child, that is necessary for the consolidation of love. Love is a three term function: man, woman, and God. Its whole perfection and success are bound up with the harmonious balance of these three elements."[14]

What could the "fall forward" have meant for Senghor if not that evolution of energies, that new vision of a creative evolution which Bergson had begun to speak of in *Time and Free Will* in 1889. Where the philosopher had remained close to the problem of the meaning of knowledge, Teilhard proceeded from a heightened and broadened grasp of the divine and could speak of a new image of the humanism of the universal. Senghor sought to find a place for the African poetical and

---

[13]Ibid., 363-64.
[14]*Human Energy*, 76.

divine vision in this new spiritual architecture which he found emerging in Claudel and later formulated in Teilhard's vision of the future.

Senghor devoted much time to Claudel's words: *ne impedias musicam* (don't hinder the music). Senghor called the poet the master of the universe after God. The poet plays his role as the musician of the world he embraces in his verse. He searches for the sounds and rhythms to bring forth the melodies of the creation; he calms the upheavals and destructions which burst forth upon and among men. We remember the work of David who would take his lyre and play when "the evil spirit of God came upon Saul...Saul would find relief and feel better, and the evil spirit would leave him" (1 Sam. 16:23). David's lyre is the poet's prosody. Here are the marvels of combinations and sounds; they return man to harmony with self and the world. Claudel wrote: "The poet who is the teacher [*magistère*] of words, and whose art is to employ them, is able by a skillful disposition of the objects which he represents, to provoke in us a harmonious and intense, just and forceful, intelligence."[15]

This state of harmonious intelligence was for both Claudel and Senghor the magisterium of the poet. With the lyre, poetry sings the rhythms and sounds which soothe man's intense anxieties about his place in the universe. Here lies the foundation of a meaningful intellectualism, one that does separate body and soul. Like David who for moments gave Saul the peace of the lyre, Claudel, who knew the majesty of the Psalms, gave back to poetry its biblical tradition, gave it the restorative powers of the soul, a divine mission. The poet is the man of belief, for like David, he says in his heart: "Safe and sound I lie down to sleep, for you alone, O Lord, keep me secure" (Ps. 4:8).

The poet feels deeply the creative power of the word. Senghor asks us not to forget that "the word does not only express intelligence in the sense of 'comprehension' and 'assimilation' of the world, it is even more a remodeling and a reconstruction of the world." He then quotes Claudel: "I will not say that you receive no lesson from nature, it is you who impose your order upon her."[16] The poet is the creator in the sense of remaker of the world. This he does not simply to restore it to a pristine paradise, but to make it truer and more harmonious. The world belongs to the future, not to the past. Its truth has only just begun to be revealed, and the poet must take the lead in showing the direction, the belief in the future, and its domination over both past and present.

The poet imposes order upon nature with the word. Again and again we hear the question resound in us: What is the marvel of the word? Is it the silent communication of the written word, the vibrant and sounding

---

[15]"La Parole chez Claudel," 367.

[16]Ibid., 370.

expression of the melodies of the spoken word? The African tradition, Senghor reminds us, has always accorded "primacy to the *spoken Word* over 'graphic signs' because the latter 'breaks the rhythm, the essence of the Word, deprives it of its force, and rends it inert, removes from it its secret by putting it at the beck and call of everyone."[17] The word is the "ontological texture of the universe," but this texture does not necessarily reveal where the universe will and can be, it only reveals what the universe is. There is a mystery between the poet's attempt to comprehend what the universe *is* and what is divine in it. The poet remains a man. The divine majesty remains beyond the beauty of the poetic ontology, but the marvel of their relationship is that they touch. The rhythms of the poet reach out to the "finger" of God.

Although Senghor speaks of the influence of Claudel, it is difficult to comprehend how he understood the quality of the influence. Claudel did not visit Africa, but had traveled widely in the Far East and the Americas. He was France's ambassador in Washington from 1927-33. Senghor explains this influence by pointing to what he believes was Claudel's Celtic temperament. "I believe," Senghor states, "that we must speak of the reemergence of the Celtic temperament.... Claudel did not renew precisely the Celtic tradition, but the Celtic temperament which is characterized by the great power of emotion and imagination."[18] These characteristics brought Claudel close to the African tradition. By identifying Claudel so closely with the Celts, he subordinated the classical and biblical traditions which played so great a role in Claudel's thought and poetry. Senghor, like every artist who approaches another, sees in him what is closest to his own soul. It would be unthinkable for Senghor not to find in the self the spiritual ties with Claudel's religiosity. Only through them could he feel the influences which Claudel had upon him. Although these influences were precious to Senghor, his interest transcended the scholarly attempt to delineate the force of influence. Senghor is a poet of humankind and what was deeply human in Claudel was necessarily human in every great tradition. Claudel deeply admired the Greek tragedies, the biblical rhythms which revealed the intimate ties between God and man, but there were also China and Japan, whose influence became part of his spirit. Senghor remarked at the end of his essay: "Whatever it may be, the convergences which I have tried to define are the certain proof of the universality of Claudel's poetry. This poetry is rooted in the body of *Man* expressing the permanent aspiration

---

[17]Ibid., 371.
[18]Ibid., 385.

of the latter toward the All-Powerful Center and the All-Animating: Loving."[19]

Deeper and more powerful than other creative human activities is the force that drives this loving and animating power about which the ancient priestess Diotima taught Socrates. Love, we know, is not a longing for beauty. It would then be a longing for death. "Love," Diotima said to Socrates, "[is] a longing not for the beautiful itself, but for the conception and generation that the beautiful effects. And why all this longing for propagation? Because this is the one deathless and eternal element in our mortality. And since we have agreed that the lover longs for the good to be his own forever, it follows that we are bound to long for immortality, as well as for the good – which is to say that Love is a longing for immortality."[20] In every aspect of Senghor's spiritual life lies this love of creation which draws him from the mortal to the immortal. In every part in which he feels the emotional powers of this love for immortality, Senghor finds a companion. Every spiritual influence that drew him toward this All-Powerful Center contributed to his capacity to look, beyond the African and French worlds, to a cosmic harmony which he sings about in his poetry. His spoken voice was also heard at conferences and ceremonies. His tranquil thoughts were written down in essays and scholarly communications. The poet seeks for the immortality that lies in his mortality, the human spirit that is called forth by the God he loves. He discovers that he becomes more and more individual as he approaches this divine attraction that animates all life.

Claudel remarked in his work in "Ma Conversion," that "the study of religion had become my dominant interest.... Little by little, slowly and painfully, it became clear to me that art and poetry are also divine things and that the pleasures of the flesh, far from being indispensable, are on the contrary, detrimental."[21] There can be little doubt that the ideas that moved Senghor were rooted in his faith in God. The deep sympathy he felt for Claudel, and then for Teilhard, emerged from a belief that could never be shaken. "Black civilization," Senghor wrote in 1974 in his introduction to the journal *Ethiopiques*, "is only an aspect of the *Civilization of the Universal* which all ethnic groups must build together or perish. It would not be human and integral if it lacked a single aspect of the human condition. *Ethiopiques* will work to build this panhuman civilization as a worker at the 'eleventh house.'"[22]

---

[19]Ibid., 386.

[20]"Symposium," trans. M. Joyce, in *The Collected Dialogues of Plato* (Princeton: Princeton University Press, 1973), 206e.

[21]"Ma Conversion," 1012, 1013.

[22]"Pourquoi *Ethiopiques*," in *Liberté* 3:563.

Senghor brings a religious feeling, an inspiration, and a love to his poetic work, and we should speak of his work as a "divine" poetry. He understood deeply what it meant to possess the image of God, to find in the word a source of creation, to show how it translates one reality into another. Diotima called love a midwife, the bringing forth of the works of love. The movement toward universality is the realization of both the individual and the particular, that striving toward that civilization of the universal that was dear to Senghor. The movement upward is created only from a movement downward. This dialogue of movements bears within it the mystery and wonders of the divine-human interplay. The poet-philosopher translates the human to the divine and the divine to the human.

Claudel described the poet with words that reveal the dialogue inherent in every creative act. "The poet," he said, "does not make use of words in the same manner [that is, in a banal manner]. He does not use them for utility but to form, from all these resonant phantoms which the word puts at our disposal, a picture that is both intelligible and delightful. Habit takes the place of the real nature of things, a second nature, a purely practical, manageable, and efficacious enemy, one which must be derailed and laid to rest as Hermes' flute long ago laid to rest the cruel Argos. The repetition of sounds, the harmony of syllables, the regularity of rhythms, and every prosodic song serve this purpose. Once the daily, working, and servile part of the soul is thus occupied and dominated, *Anima* freely advances in the midst of pure things with an infinitely light and rapid step."[23]

We conclude with this description because we believe that the capacity to form a vision of the world requires an understanding of man's spiritual purpose in the world, and an even deeper comprehension and embrace of the creative act. The world is given to man on many levels and can be spiritually grasped on each of them. Man's understanding both of himself and of God are just beginning to be revealed. We have overcome the naive notion of a fixed harmony, of a limited cosmos. Truth has become mutability and evolution. The dynamics of an evolving universe, drawn by the love of God, overwhelms the imagination. It forces it to form new images and symbols.

Senghor's relationship to the great figures of French literature and poetry reflects the need of the soul to live with a particular tradition and language and, at the same time, to transform and transfigure this tradition through the influences and forms of others. We have arrived at that philosophy of *métissage* (mixture) that has always been precious to

---

[23]"Lettre à l'Abbé Brémond sur l'inspiration poétique," in *Oeuvres en prose, 48.*

Senghor. Peoples belong to each other, their roots are intertwined with those of innumerable other peoples. It is in this *métissage* that people find strength and creativity. From his fellow poets, Senghor found the powers of metamorphoses, these divine powers which makes man a cocreator of the universe. Senghor sings of man's glory and also of his burden. He sings of a creative love that causes man to move from body to spirit and then again from spirit to body. He chants the ode that every man listens to and understands in his humanity: the ode to fraternity.

6

A Beautiful Picture: The Embrace of Senghor, Chagall, and Bachelard

The philosopher Gaston Bachelard (1884-1962) was a rare and unique thinker who cultivated man's right to dream, who sought to explore the images, the metaphors, and reveries which gave to man and to his history a quality of wonder and adventure allowed to no other being. Bachelard was the philosopher of poetic reverie. He ventured into the depths of the imagination, seeking to find the common experience that he believed linked mankind: the wonder that dwells in every being who is struck by the powers that live in imagery, that communicates with the elements and the dreams they engender in him. Man dreams the infinite varieties of forms that appear to him in the sensory objects he uses and grasps with fascination and fantasy. It is this fascination that brings man to realms of imagination which he could only anticipate in hope and excitement. Here man is open to a freedom of thinking and imagining which causes others to shudder, and some to withdraw in bewilderment. Bachelard not only reflected upon the formation of images, but showed us how, before every natural phenomenon, man became a dreamer. He could be lifted to new realms of reality, to new creative forms. In these he found the source of science, literature, and poetry.

I have often wondered why Senghor never mentioned this philosopher of the *Poetics of Reverie,* why his name remained unspoken. There is a feeling that much of what Bachelard said and wrote quietly became a part of Senghor's philosophical attitude and poetry. We read in Senghor the names of many thinkers of the 1930s and 1940s, we see references to Valéry, Saint-John Perse, Bergson, Maritain, Mounier, Berger, Teilhard. But Bachelard is referred to just once. We will refer to him. Through the magic of his thought we will direct his light upon Senghor. In this light we will see their relationship, the closeness that comes from men who do not openly recognize each other, but in their silence find their way to each other.

In 1938 Bachelard published his widely read book *The Psychoanalysis of Fire*. He reminded us that "fire is a privileged phenomenon which explains anything. If all that changes slowly may be explained by life, all that changes quickly is explained by fire. Fire is the ultra-living element. It is intimate. It is universal. It lives in our heart. It lives in the sky. It rises from the depths of the substance and offers itself with the warmth of love. Or it can go back down into the substance and hide there, latent and pent-up, like hate and vengeance."[1] We turn to a culture to find and describe the sources of its art, literature, and religion, and we compare one culture with the other, but there are the universal elements, the substances which bear in them marvels of imagery, dream, and reverie. Here we find a dimension of life that is different from the reason which organizes and forms its materials, seeks the truth of relationships, or the truth of their absence. In science, the mind dominates and molds its matter into forms which it believes it controls. In the depths of subjectivity, there lie other powers, those that we ascribe to the imagination, powers we don't control, but which are only subsequently grasped and revealed. The imagination causes us to realize how spontaneous is the imagery that emerges from us. We live with an indeterminateness that fascinates our being and thinking. We see ourselves as the children not only of reason, but of the creative image as well. We are men of wonder, finding in it the source of our thinking and imagination.

This wonder links all men to a universe of spiritual creativity. It is at this point that Senghor goes beyond the phenomenon of wonder, beyond our attempt to explore its infinite forms and possibilities, to give to reality a universal spiritual realm in which this phenomenon becomes the expression and dimension of a universal humanism, a civilization of the universal. Senghor carefully enunciated this universal spiritual view. He stated: "In this last quarter of the twentieth century, the Dialogue of Cultures has begun to exert its dominance. This cultural revolutionary movement was born in the pains of conquests, massacres, deportations, heightened by the hazards of voyages, of partitions and treaties. Now the question is to organize in rational and human ways, that is, through a dialogue in which each race, nation, civilization, receives and gives at the same time, and each will be able through self-development to expand in his person."[2] In Senghor, the philosophy of subjectivity, poetically

[1]*The Psychoanalysis of Fire* (Boston: Beacon Press, 1964), 7.

[2]*Négritude et Civilization de l'Universel,* in *Liberté* (Paris: Editions du Seuil, 1977), 3:20.

announced by Bachelard, becomes a meditation on universality, a vision of dialogues, allowing men to approach cultures that are different from their own and feel the quality of that "cosmic egg" in which the elements of earth and heaven are gathered together. "From Leda and the Swan, an egg is born, for every great vision of the world must start with the cosmic egg.... The man who enjoys the demiurgic power of modeling goes all the way in exploring the forces that are born in the substances of the earth."[3]

This demiurgic power, this force of modeling, belongs to man universally, and it is through this realization that we become aware of how profound are the differences and similarities among cultures. If Bachelard gave us the impression that there is a universal imagination, that we are all addressed by the elements of air, water, fire, that the flame of a candle brings forth innumerable images, then he is assuming that this universal imaginative power is similar in various cultures, and that through them we can approach a humanism that reveals demiurgic reality. We are beginning to see that the wonders of man belong to this forging and modeling capacity which surpasses all other characteristics. Man, the maker and thinker, brings together imagination and thinking, but he doesn't identify them. He knows that they relate to each other, but remain distinct and individual. Fusion would make it possible for them to exert their unique forces, but would weaken their capacities to function. Yet they are spiritual companions. Each knows the lights of wonder and awe, but each creates differently and distinctly.

Nothing makes us more aware of the self than "the objective knowledge of the *subjective.*" We don't place subjectivity and objectivity one against each other. We seek to know and feel the depths and forces of subjectivity, realizing that these are the original sources of the self, that they are the objects living in the subject, making it both object and subject. We move toward this subject "where we discover in our own heart the human universal, when, after having honestly psychoanalyzed our study of the self, we integrate the rules of morality with laws of psychology. Then the fire which was consuming us, suddenly enlightens us. The haphazard passion becomes the deliberate passion. Love becomes family; fire becomes hearth and home."[4]

The more we think of Bachelard and Senghor, the more we realize that in this silent conversation between poet and philosopher there is an intimacy that draws one naturally to the other. Senghor dreams of universality, of dialogues, and of exchanges. His vision is that of Africa emerging into a world that has only begun to comprehend Africa's

---

[3]Gaston Bachelard "Henri de Waroquier, Sculptor: Man and His Destiny," in *The Right to Dream* (New York: Grossman Publishers, 1972), 39-40.
[4]*The Psychoanalysis of Fire,* 101.

spiritual life. Africa is a continent plundered and tortured, living with hate, but wanting to give and receive. This is a continent consumed and enlightened by those who came to profit financially, but who would in turn be enlightened by those they sought to exploit. From the movement of slavery to freedom would develop others which would bring equality and mutuality. "I know," Senghor remarked, "that the treatment of the Negroes was the heavy tribute of the deported, but, above all, of the deaths of tens of millions which Africa had to pay to hurry along the movement [of the Civilization of the Universe]. Doubtlessly, the immense holocaust of black victims was useless, but such is the hard law of history. Every truth of a new civilization is made in pain and blood."[5]

We read these words with astonishment and sadness. We agree with the common opinion that birth is pain, but we have morally struggled to lessen that pain, to cry out against those who inflict it arbitrarily and for personal aggrandizement. In Senghor, there is no prophetic voice that cries out against man's inhumanity to man if in the course of time and events a new era would be born and the "good news" would be announced. We know that we do not redo the past and that judgments about it from the present are always inadequate, but we cannot help forming images of suffering and degradation. The moral outrage is not only a condemnation, but the creation of the moral world which for generations has gathered strength from the prophets' fantasies of hopes and courage. We regret that Senghor let the "hard law of history" deprive us of the overwhelming images that we derive from moral wrong. In this respect, the poet has failed us.

Bachelard may seem to be nonpolitical. It is only when we read his introduction to Chagall's *Bible*, when we listen to his reactions to the paintings of the prophets, to figures such as Joel and Zechariah, that we find the depths of moral wonderment, that tremendous volcanic feeling that emerges in reaction to the prophet's call for justice, for Israel's rectitude, and for the world mission of humanity. If, at first glance, Bachelard appears to skirt the political, if he doesn't envision images such as the universal dialogue, if he doesn't share the dreams of Teilhard, there is nevertheless a sense of the political in that incomprehensible freedom that is the source of man's imaginative powers. The political is the guarantor of the right to dream, to wonder. It bears witness in tranquillity to man's unconquerable need to be imaginative, to describe the images and dreams that proceed from his contemplation and meditation upon the elements of nature and the creative acts of man. We need to be free of political and religious

---

[5]*Négritude et Civilization de l'Universel*, in *Liberté* (Paris: Editions du Seuil, 1977), 3:9.

orthodoxies, of ideologies, and of the oppressive weight of a past that can no longer be opened to a future, that doesn't allow for wonder, and denies to man what is novel and different. Bachelard is a political being in a way that allows him to hold in awe the sacred powers of dreams as man's most precious gifts, those which allow him to absorb the light like the facades of Monet's cathedrals gather the light. Senghor also sends forth messages which become visions for the world, dreams which few understand or take seriously. The philosopher-poet adores the unfathomable subject which every being experiences, but few explore with eager concern. He exalts the precious word which he calls poetry.

We have always known. We have deeply felt. We have imagined that the world asks to be seen, not seen with fleeting glances, momentary glimpses, but with an embrace, a love, and a need for communication. "The world asks to be seen," remarked Bachelard, "before ever there were eyes to see the eye of the waters, the huge eye of still waters watched the flowers bloom, and it was in this reflection – who will deny it – that the world became aware of its beauty." The artist is the "guide of the forces of beauty that direct the world." Bachelard refers to the water lilies of Claude Monet, who knew how to tell "the brief and burning story of the flowers of the river."[6] If there is a beauty that directs the world, then we are all part of the grand endeavor to search for this beauty, to pass beyond the reality that captures our daily existence. We need to find that light which illumines our cavelike habits. The world asks to be seen. We need to learn how to see it as we learn how to hear and smell, touch and embrace it. The philosopher muses among these images of the senses. He explores the realm of man's wonders. In them he discovers the dreams that excite and exalt humankind, the dreams men require to give nobility to life. Man not only searches for the riddles of existence, but he longs for those imaginary jolts that happily deprive life of an ordered symmetry that has been put together by a preconceived logic or an arbitrary definition of the purpose of life.

We bear within ourselves the forces of a tradition whose impulses and subtleties we hardly encompass with our reason, which leave us with a stream of images we refuse to leave in the hands of those who like to form fixed patterns of meaning. We recall a short and poignant poem of Senghor that speaks of these images, a poem called "Totem":

> I must hide him in my intimate veins
> My Ancestor with the flesh of bright thunder and skin of fire
> My animal protector, I must hide him
> Lest I snap through the doors of shame
> He is my faithful blood who requires faith

---

[6]"Water Lilies or Surprises of a Summer's Dawn," in *The Right to Dream*, 6-7.

Guarding my naked pride against
Myself and the scorn of the blessed tribes...[7]

We feel the worlds that are bound in us, which pulsate through our being, that determine our fate and demand our faith. We don't only ask their meaning, we strive to encompass their reality, to make them part of our being, finding ourselves more deeply immersed in their imagery. My reverie, the poetics of this reverie, make me a demiurgic power which allows me to recreate and perpetually form new relationships, to find new dialectical movements between life and death, birth and rebirth, and experience that awesome metamorphosis to which all reality is given as the source of its existence.

We read the poet, we meditate with the philosopher, and we slowly, and at times, suddenly, come to the realization that together they take us on a grand voyage through lands of the imagination, showing us how infinite are the creative possibilities that live in the man who touches the beauty that guides the world. Senghor's dreams lie in the magic and marvel of words. For those who have rarely tasted these forces, there is only skepticism and mockery. Are your words, says the skeptic, nothing more than fanciful expressions invented to overcome the immediacies of life? Did *Guernica*, says the disdainer of art, ever make a convert to anti-Fascism? These questions hover over us and will be perpetually asked. We know that we are dreamers, as well as skeptics. This is a relationship which cannot be avoided. We have "a right to dream."

We have a need to be skeptical. Do we need a resolution of this contract or only a living together of forces that nourish each other, but don't necessarily forge a symmetrical whole? Thinking and imagining need the freedom of indeterminism, of jolts, of inconclusiveness to develop the sporadic, but natural, forms of creativity. Indeterminism is the source of creative thinking. It is the divine act.

Let us add another figure to this dialogue between Bachelard and Senghor, the painter Marc Chagall. Chagall visited Dakar in 1971 for an exhibition of his paintings. Senghor spoke on the occasion. Bachelard wrote an "Introduction to Chagall's *Bible*" (1960), some of which was later reprinted in *The Biblical Message of Marc Chagall* (1973). We begin with an autobiographical note from Bachelard. "Reading alone to myself and meditating on the Bible, I used to find the voice so powerful that I could not always see the Prophet. For me all the Prophets had the voice of Prophecies. Now, as I look at the plates in this beautiful volume, I read the ancient book in a different way. I hear more clearly because I can see

[7]Selected Poems/Poésies Choisies Léopold Sédar Senghor (London: Rex Collings, 1976), 42. See also *The Collected Poetry* (Charlottesville and London: University of Virginia, 1991), 14.

more clearly, because the seer Chagall has depicted the voice that speaks. Chagall, in fact, has shone a light in my ear." The light is a "messenger of infinite mysteries."[8] We notice in this dialogue of cultures that we are speaking of more than conversations, or conferences of worldwide organizations. We speak of what Novalis called the silent powers of the night, the tranquil messages that cultures give to each other as they reveal the inner journeys of their soul. From the night comes the cry of the poet who knows its tranquillity, who feels its comfort and the union which we sense in its dark majesty. The poet Senghor calls forth the need for this comforting darkness in his poem "Prayer to Masks":

> Let's raise the cry, Here! Now! to the rebirth of the world
> Like the heaven which the white flour needs
> For who would teach rhythms to a world blasted by machines
> and guns?
> Who would carry the joy-cry to waken the dead and the
> orphaned at dawn?
> Say, who would bring life's memory back to the men of gutted
> hopes?
> They call us the men of cotton, of coffee, of oil,
> They call us the waking dead.
> But we are the men of the dance whose feet draw power in
> beating the solid ground.[9]

We seek the cry that shakes our daily existence, that reaches from the earth to the heavens, from darkness to light, and from light to darkness. We search for a world that needs to be heard and seen, that needs the man who lives from the earth and reaches forth toward the heaven. We journey toward the biblical man who stood, gazed, and felt the ladder of Jacob, experiencing the upward movement in the downward, knowing that he can draw the heavens to the earth and the earth to the heavens, realizing the light in the darkness and the darkness in the light.

Man loves the world which he knows how to see. The world approaches his listening and his touching. It comes to him in the love which these senses embody. It is encompassed by them and it is created through them. Love finds its vehicles in the senses and with them it recreates the reality around it. In love there is joy which both the painter and the poet embrace in their words and their colors. Their feelings and emotions arise from what they see and hear. They watch and meditate on the sounds and images that appear to them. We hear their words. Their light and darkness open our ears. Senghor exclaims in "These Roads of Insomnia":

> I cry the full joy flooding my heart like the rain-swollen Niger

[8]"Introduction to Chagall's *Bible*," in *The Right to Dream*, 8-9.
[9]*Selected Poems*, 41.

Joy to the beasts of the mangroves – *Listen*!
Joy to the couples who chatter on straw-matter sand – Listen![10]

This joy that fills my heart announces the love that I find in my sensory world, a world close to the creation and not disemboweled by the abstractions of reason, hurrying toward an abstract divinity. When we learn to listen and to see, we go beyond our immediate experience, we learn to find a world of representations that no longer reflects the needs and satisfactions of our favorite objects. The world expands through the instruments of our love and in this expansion we rediscover the traces of the divine. We discover how the divine lives in our senses.

Bachelard remarked that "everything is paradise to the eye that knows how to look and loves seeing." "Chagall," he said, "loves the world because he knows how to look at it, and even more because he has learned how to portray it. Paradise is the world of beautiful colors.... Paradise is first and foremost a beautiful picture."[11] We regard the figures. We are impressed with the colors and we realize, like Bachelard, that they are words. Colors are words; they don't tell us about this or that object, but they cause us to wonder, to allow images to come forth, to think about the imaginative power in us that bursts forth in imagery and refuses to be limited by purpose or immediate significance. Suddenly, we are aware that the figures and the colors have stories to tell, ones that we may record at the moment, knowing that the stories are endless, and that what is said is only the beginning of what will be said. But we are joyful that we can begin the telling of the story, that we can describe the ineffable with representations, that what we see in the painting *Paradise* is the story of mankind revealing its primordial forms. "These paintings," Chagall reminded us, "as I conceived them, do not represent the dream of one particular people, but of all mankind.... If every life drifts ineluctably toward its end, we must color ours while it lasts with our own colors of love and hope. The social logic of life and the essence of every religion is founded upon this love. For me, perfection in art and life spring forth from the biblical source. The mere mechanics of logic and constructiveness cannot produce any fruit in art, as in life without this spirit."[12]

Men will come to Chagall's paintings and dream. Some will say to them as the brothers said to Joseph: Here comes the dreamer. But this right to dream is the essence of man's faith, it is the substance of his courage and hope, his freedom and creativity. If art serves a divine

---

[10]Ibid., 107.
[11]"Introduction to Chagall's *Bible*," 9.
[12]*The Biblical Message of Marc Chagall* (New York: Tudor Publishing Co., 1972), 15-16.

purpose, it is to call forth man's dreams, to allow him to form them in the words and wonders of color, in parables and tales. If we think for a moment of Senghor and Bachelard, of the poet and the philosopher, we encounter dreamers, men who have brought together the reality of the senses and of the mind, but who have been open to those unknown illuminations which flow from above and give us new visions of what is here below. Man, the creator, feels the powers of love, he knows that in art as in life, "all is possible if conceived in love." Childish are man's ways when he inquires about the meaning of love. He turns to the priestess Diotima with innocence and openness and awaits the words of the ancient prophetess. She is the teacher of creation in beauty and love. With similar openness, we turn to the artist and regard the paintings that have flowed from his creations in love. "Creating quickly," Bachelard stated, "is the secret of creating life. Life will not wait; life never stops to think. No rough drafts, just flashes. All Chagall's creatures are first flashes."[13] These are secrets we all search for in everything we do and hope. We are voyagers with inner journeys to make, and with these we want to become a part of humankind. "I would like," Chagall noted, "their music and their heartfelt poetry to be heard."[14]

We feel the sense of exaltation as we gaze upon *Paradise*. We stand before a creator of color and forms and we wonder at the paradise that man has never sought to yield, believing himself to be the cocreator with God. This sense of exaltation and creation fills both the poet and the philosopher. Encountering both *Paradise* and *Adam and Eve Being Chased from Paradise* reveals to us the delights and the tragedy of the senses. We enter a realm of seeing and hearing that we never imagined to be possible. Music speaks its words in sounds. From it we learn to listen. Painting speaks in colors. We learn to see. "What a privilege for a creator of forms," Bachelard stated, "who is also a painter of genius to be called on to depict paradise! Yet surely all is paradisical to an eye that truly sees and delights in seeing. Chagall loves the visible. He knows how to look at it, and, above all, he has learned to depict it. Paradise is a world of beautiful colors, and for a painter to invent a new approach to color, is a paradisical thrill. He conjures up something he does not see; in other words, he creates."[15]

We meet the power in which all creation is possible: love. In love we believe everything of beauty is possible. The love of the creation was shared by Senghor, Chagall, and Bachelard. From wherever it came, and in whatever form it appeared, it revealed a sense of parturition and

---

[13]"Introduction to Chagall's *Bible*," 10.
[14]*The Biblical Message*, 16.
[15]Ibid., 23.

intimacy. Man discovers these rare feelings of oneness with the creation. This oneness assumes multiple forms which each being discovers in sound, color, thought, and imagination. The world asks to be created again and again, but even this request has its limitation. Man, to remain the lover, must be radically different from God, who can only proclaim himself to man as: I am who I will eternally be. Man needs to journey to places of discovery; he is forever attempting to find his essence. Man is the being in search of the love that creates his love.

"Every tree of the garden you are free to eat; but as for the tree of knowledge of good and bad, you must not eat of it; for as soon as you eat of it you shall die" (Gen. 2:15). In paradise lies temptation. Only in this way could paradise be for man, could it be comprehensible to him. God, in tempting man, becomes the judge; he gives man a history from which man forms the idea of humankind and learns to approach God again as the being of temptation, the being driven from paradise but who has never forgotten it and for whom it remains a vision, a hope, and a need. When the gates of paradise were closed, the destiny of Israel began. "Henceforth," Bachelard remarked, "the gates of Paradise are closed. The old Testament is a grandiose record of the destinies of mankind, of the Fall. The Prophets tell the story of the great destiny of one group of people: the destiny of Israel."[16]

With the closing of the gates many stories begin. The God of wrath encompasses his people with judgment that is stern and compassionate. Man learns to sing of both his justice and his love. Man begins his travels into memories. He creates art and literature, but above all, his moral visions. The closing of the gates is a fascinating and magical metaphor of a world that ended, but has never ended, a world that is yet to come and will always be in the future. It is an image from which a vast number of images flow forth. We never forget the closing of the gates because it is always present. We are excited and exalted by the new world, the coming kingdom of God's compassion. We dream of the new light, the metaphor that is yet to be realized. There is the closing of the gates, the wrath of God, and our sense of guilt. These pictures will never depart from us, they remain our destiny. From them, the lost paradise never reemerges, but we need a paradise. We remain with the voices of the prophets who are scandalized by our actions, but promise redemption, a search for a "new heart." Man's story is a tale of struggle, of persistence and defeat, of progress and retrogression. The crucible of fire becomes the redeeming balm of strength and vision. We remain lost without answers. But we remember that no answers were ever promised. None will ever be given.

---

[16]Ibid., 27.

Chagall's *Message* is a meditation. It commands our imagination, forces us to dream, a phenomenon that never ceases to arouse our feeling of freedom. The paintings take us in many directions; they speak to us from many perspectives and sources. We realize that they only address us when we are capable of hearing and seeing what they have to say. The seeing is possible only when receptivity is able to absorb what is given. So much more can be received if we are drawn toward the colors and the forms, if our eyes learn to see and our ears listen to what is silently being said. This tranquil communication fascinates and fondles our senses, entices them to go beyond themselves and see what is not seen and hear what is not heard. "Do not leaf through the book," Bachelard admonishes us, "leave it open at one page that speaks to you. You will become caught up in one of the great dreams of temporality; you will come to know the musings of the millennia. Chagall will teach you how to be five or six thousand years old.... We must dream and dream a great deal – dream in the knowledge that life is a dream, that what one dreams over and above what he has lived is real, vital, there, present, in all truth, before our eyes."[17]

We ponder the realm of dreaming. It is the realm of creating. We don't understand what it is to create. We think more often of re-creating, of adding on, reliving, giving new form to what is already there and receptive to what we do. We believe that reality is there to be molded and brought forth. It is ready to be born. We learn that love is birth in beauty. Plato taught us how to mount the ladder from body to spirit, from one form to another in an endless chain toward the light, toward the One which illumines everything, which we only slowly and hesitantly approach. But the light not only illumines, it causes us to dream of the vast spiritual possibilities that lie in human life. The imagination is free to wonder, to seek that world of images in which we discover the powers of the imagination. When we discover that sensitivity to appearances, we realize that the path of wonder is open to us. The poet, the painter, the musician show us the ways of love and what lies in them. We need not only fleeting appearances, but those that have become a part of our history, that are now our destiny. The past, with the remembrances that consume it, attempts to know the present and to reveal the future to its source. We are capable of living in time by reaching out to the past with fascination, contemplating, at the same time, the future with hope. The past flows into the present with a "destinal energy." In these two words, we feel an excitement that makes us part of the living history whose reality is only beginning to be understood. This history belongs to our wonder. It harbors no answers

[17]"Introduction to Chagall's *Bible*," 12.

but only meditations and paintings. We are sad to learn how few solutions are offered to us through either history or philosophy. We have only to wonder.

"What does history matter to me," Bachelard said, "now that the past is present, now that a past that is not mine has taken root in my soul, producing dream after endless dream?"[18] Bachelard realized that history was not a chronology of events, a series of causes and effects; it was a panorama of human actions filled with stories which capture and entice the soul, which cause us flights of imagination, which allow us not only to think, to understand, but also to dream. The closing of the gates of paradise, the chase from paradise, are inexhaustible dreams, dramas of reverie that overwhelm the reason and subject it to wonderment and awe. We are beyond the concept and the idea, no rationality can embrace the closing of the gates. We are left adrift, struggling with reason to give us meaning where there are only images, where metamorphosis takes on startling reality. The past rushes toward the present and the future glances into the destiny of both. Time is transfigured into eternity in paradise; all its divisions fade away and we encounter a cosmic reality: a divine-human harmony. We yearn to bring back this inner peace we have lost, but it remains only a memory lost in the past, but vitally present. We remember the chase from paradise and we think of the stories it engendered, stories of humankind, told by the waywardness of man and the stern finger of God's judgment. Love has merged into justice, but we long for it in every act and relationship. The tree of the knowledge of good and evil was not for man. Our demonic curiosity destroyed our ignorance. We fell prey to our inordinate desire to be God. Paradise is an eternal reality. Like its sequel, the chase from paradise, it reveals the ever presence of an eternal history that absorbs within itself the past, the present, and the future.

This history is told through visions and dreams. It is told with a reality which assures us that there is a realm of forms beyond those we see and hear in our encounter with the reality about us. The poet-painter takes us on a journey that surpasses history, that emerges into new tales of metamorphosis, of transfigured reality, of cosmic harmony. "Contradicting history," the critic Robert Marteau remarked, "utilizing it and passing beyond it, with seeming effortlessness, Chagall devotes all his effort to restoring the full meaning to the words of the legend, to what should be read, told, recounted, shown, taught. He is a navigator along the invisible border between the here and the beyond, a walker on air; he treads the skies, the prairies, and the seas which the poor clouds hide from us, and he steps on them in order to make a stepping stone for

---

[18]Ibid., 12-13.

the figures who populate this invisible place and through whom he gives full vent to his feelings."[19]

Chagall appears before us as "a prophet like fire, whose word flamed like a torch" (Eccles. 48:1-12). His colors consume and transfigure, his forms lead us to new paths and we are exalted with the imagination which flows from us. We are caught in a "fiery whirlwind" and feel swept away into new realms of being. But here we are grasped by the poetry of colors, words that teach us how to see and hear. We are awakened to a reality where Senghor, Bachelard, and Chagall are joined as companions in this dialogue of dreams. We envision a new symposium in which three companions speak of dreams. They are our great dreamers. Humankind is ennobled because of them.

The dreams embrace man's wish that his universe will be changed morally. "The entire universe, animals, men and things," Bachelard remarked, "is destined to be uplifted."[20] This vision belongs intimately to Senghor. Beyond the reality of Negritude, the poet never left the images and beliefs of Teilhard de Chardin. He could feel the grandeur of the prophets, men who were deeply aware of the reality about them, the corruption and idolatry of kings, the voices of the false prophets, but never could their visions be lessened and turned to skepticism. This enduring faith is the mark of the great moral figure. If we were challenged to find greatness in Senghor's life, we would turn to that remarkable courage of spirit which made it possible for him to encounter the evil of men and governments and still believe in the goodness and progress of humankind. We turn with wonder to this "divine" strength and courage, this undaunted faith, and think of the words of Zechariah: "Not by might, nor by power, but by My Spirit, said the Lord of Hosts" (Zech. 4:6). The dream that the spirit shall subdue the sword belongs to that universality of dialogue that Senghor cherished.

The poet speaks too well for a pessimist, the artist draws too well for a skeptic. The philosopher attempts to communicate the effects of these forms upon the mind and the feelings. He wants to show us the reverie that emerges from the work of the spirit, how we are drawn to the sources of imagery and dream. Chagall, Bachard stated, "trusts his pencil; he has confidence in his brush, and so the world is beautiful. The universe is worthy to be painted. It feels good, it is good to belong to a world that is beautiful. The joy of painting is a joy in living. The universe – Chagall's illustrations are the proof of this – is destined, above and beyond all misery, to happiness. Man must regain Paradise."[21] There is a

---

[19]Comment of Robert Marteau in *Biblical Message*, 170.
[20]"Introduction to Chagall's *Bible*," 22.
[21]Ibid.

spiritual fraternity among the painter, the poet, and the philosopher. They know that the universe has much to reveal to man, that the creative spirit is man's most precious gift. The gift is inexhaustible. Men must find the bridges that will bring cultures to each other, but they must, above all, find a way to their own culture.

In his speech at the opening of the Chagall's exposition in Dakar, Senghor spoke of the character of Chagall's work, of the Russian and biblical tradition, the rejection of cubism and the positive force of surrealism. Even more important than those sensitive reflections were Senghor's concluding words. They reflect the universality of vision: "We are here involved in a *new humanism.* It is significant that the exile, Marc Chagall, who deeply suffered because of race and religion, remained without hate. If he sketched, engraved, painted poverty and suffering, he most often gave us hope and happiness in the fraternity of men. The Wolof proverb says: Man is the remedy for man."[22] This absence of hate is the miracle of the great man. How well he knows the evil of man, how thoughtfully he has observed reality. When he meditates on paradise and the closing of the gates of paradise, he can do nothing but see and hear the harmony of a moment becoming the disharmony of another. He hears the words of Cain: "Am I my brother's keeper?" and he lets the words become a fiery mood of accusation bearing witness to man's waywardness and cruelty.

We listen to the ideas and images that flow in upon us and we want to adhere to them in comfort, but we find an uneasiness and want to let them float about us. Comfort makes us uneasy. The encircling forms and figures attract and entice us, but we cannot seize them and demonstrate their validity. We are distressed with our incapacity to find tranquillity in fluidity. Bachelard, at the end of a posthumous work on the poetics of fire, spoke of this reality that could not be defined but only described: "The man who meditates says to the shower of images: 'What do you hide from me by showing me this image? Who shows does not demonstrate. Who demonstrates disdains to show.' The more brilliant the image the more troubling is its ambiguity, the ambiguity of the depths. Honest people wish the image to be superficial and ephemeral. A water that runs on an immobile sand, a water which in its flow reflects a distant sky.... But the sky and the earth together give to the image its verticality. Everything that mounts conceals the forces of profundity."[23] The images of verticality link the spirit to the body, reveal the precious dependence that one has upon the other. But they are not necessarily

---

[22]"Marc Chagall et l'art nègre," in *Liberté* (Paris: Editions du Seuil, 1977), 3:260.

[23]*Fragments d'une poétique du feu* (Paris: Presses Universitaires de France, 1988), 173.

arranged as the below and the above. The images float about raising the body into spirit. The spirit and the body become one to our sight, yet they are always separate from each other. We are aware that this separation is both true and unreal, necessitated by habit and speech. Through the dream, we again join the body to the spirit, revealing the oneness that makes each a part of the other.

We feel the oneness that lives in diversity, that coincidence of opposites that belongs not to logic, but to the experience of life. When Senghor spoke of Chagall's art "as flowing, subtle and iridescent, fragrant and smiling, tender and delicate," he pointed to its contrast with African art that is "austere and rude, direct and rhythmic."[24] The contrast revealed a consciousness that bears within it a multiplicity of views. Each is a divine way, nourished from the tradition and its history, each needs to communicate its substance and draw to itself the traditions of others. This giving and receiving is the dialogue of cultures which is precious. Senghor, in his introduction to the first volume of *Liberté* (1964), stated a position which I believe he never compromised, but through the years enhanced and exalted: "Let the reader," he said, "read with a fraternal spirit the pages that follow. Such would be our message. If there is race, and we cannot deny it, then the one that here speaks is a voice without hate. We have forgotten all that we could. Two hundred million died from the treatment of the Negroes, from the violence of the Conquest, the humiliations of the natives as a whole. We have retained from all this only the positive consequences. We have been the grain crushed underfoot, the grain which dies in order that a new Civilization may arise on the scale of the integral Man."[25]

We encounter this amazing theological view of history in which redemption and suffering are brought together in such a way that each becomes a divine force necessary for the realization of the vision of a new world order that comes forth from the words of the prophet Amos: "To Me, O Israelites, you are just like the Ethiopians." For this world order suffering and redemption become the forces that create humankind. Again and again Senghor turns from immediate realities to speak of the future, to speak the message of the past, to enunciate his religious faith. This turning toward a religious view of humankind makes it possible for Senghor to go beyond what is African and French. He is now the voice and conscience of humanity. Like Samuel, he hears the voice. It is this voice he must clarify. Its message needs to be given to man. The poet, the

---

[24]"Marc Chagall et L'art Nègre" in *Négritude et Civilization de l'Universel,* in *Liberté* (Paris: Editions du Seuil, 1977), 3:260.

[25]*Négritude et Civilization de l'Universel,* in *Liberté* (Paris: Editions du Seuil, 1977), 1:9.

philosopher, the painter must follow the path of Joel and blow a horn and gather the people, exhorting the people to a new dialogue. The bird, as Chagall showed, will carry the flowers of peace in its beak, it is the harbinger of the angel who will come. We will know that the spirit will be upon all flesh. Senghor dreams dreams. These are the realities we want to hear from him. With his dreams, he brings us courage and hope. He brings the words of redemption to a suffering humanity.

7

Senghor Discovers Spiritual Companionship in Personalism

We have little reason to believe that ideas such as humanity belong necessarily to the history of human evolution. In fact, man's spiritual creations can be assumed to be accidental and tangential. They are held to be hypothetical and created in belief. The more we realize how contingent the Idea is, the more we grasp its grandeur. If the Idea was a necessary consequence of man's increasing intelligence and aptitudes, we would find little reason to recognize it with astonishment and awe. We wonder about the creation of poetry, philosophy, music, painting, and science because we find in them extraordinary and unexpected powers of human ingenuity. We put aside causes and events which satisfy our need for explanation and definition, because we know that there are no causes or events that *explain* the creative act, although we find influences of culture, religion, and history. We are enamored with the intellect, the will, and the marvels that abide in creativity. They lift us above the daily course of events They show us the powers of change, of transfiguration and transformation.

We bring this about in the world, which we create in thinking. The marvel of the person fascinates us because it liberates us from the individual. The person is the embodiment, the microcosm of intellectual, moral, and volitional activities which reflect the unique substance of man's place in the universe. Man is more than the individual who is free to wander the world in search of unending meaning and purpose.

The more he wanders, the more he is conscious of the loneliness of his individuality. Man's wandering is in the self, the experience of the self, the confrontation with an inner life that is rich in possibilities and hopes. It is intimate contact with intellect, will, and hope. The individual becomes person as he becomes more deeply aware of his relationship to transcendence and self-realization. The individual is constantly discovering the spiritual aloneness of the self. The person is never freed from task and obligation, from dialogue and community. The individual goes in search of his daily bread, the person asks for his daily hunger.

Great philosophy has always sought to discover the nature of the person. It always finds the violence of anarchic individualism, the torturous consequences of collectivist materialism, and the painful destructiveness of racism and totalitarianism. At every stage of human history we face the violence that denatures the person and which, at the same time, gives him the capacity to overcome this violence.

In 1932, the first issue of one of the most significant journals devoted to the person, *Esprit,* appeared, under the guidance of the philosopher Emmanuel Mounier (1905-50). The whys and the wherefores lay in the spiritual need of the time. What we know is that men need spiritual communication. It speaks to their intellectual and practical realities. These realities have always escaped conceptualization and definitional determination. They express man's freedom, the unknown, undefinable and unknowable. These realities form our essence, although they remain unknown in their essence. We know that there dwells in us a realm of reality which we do not dominate, but seek to comprehend. It rents space within us but refuses to be our servants. It is divine gift and a "golden bough."

The first issue of *Esprit* appeared in 1932 with an explicatory manifesto called "Refaire la Renaissance" (Let Us Remake the Renaissance). Jean Lacroix, a member of the editorial board, explained its meaning: "What we call a spiritualist attitude is giving to the word spiritualism its true meaning. The most common error is to confuse spirituality with inwardness, by considering the spirit as some unknown substance without relationship to the rest of reality. To become spiritual is often, in the ordinary sense of the word, to turn in upon the self. This is not our meaning. The soul and the body are tied. The personalist revolution is an integral one. We have said and repeated it often: True man is only partially adaptable, he seeks and wants beyond what he has, and beyond what he is. This fundamental inadaptability is doubtlessly the definition of the human being as body and spirit."[1]

We are at a position that takes us back to Socrates, to the intelligence that warns us that an unexamined life is not worth living, and that human conversation and action depend upon the desire to converse, and the need to act. We are men only to the degree that we are capable of entering into dialogue both with ourselves and with others. We need no dialogue when we feel the certainty of our intelligence and the indisputability of our will. We need dialogue when we realize that we

---

[1]Jean Lacroix, *Le Personnalisme* (Lyon: Chronique Sociale, 1981), 129.

depend upon community both for knowledge and for political and moral activity. With these preliminary remarks, we can imagine the affinity that Senghor felt for Mounier and *Esprit*. Here was a Christian philosopher who would again speak to the person, the bearer of the image of God, and who would stress the power of dialogue as the source of community, not only for individuals and groups, but for nations and cultures. A group of intellectuals led by Mounier attempted to combat the devastating forces of totalitarianism with a journal that proclaimed the message of the Prophet Zechariah: "Not by might, nor by power, but by My Spirit, said the Lord of Hosts" (Zech. 4:6).

Where there is the possibility for dialogue, we have subdued, but not eliminated the power of violence. Lacroix noted that there is dialogue only where there is belief in humanity. "The man of dialogue is the one who wants to join the extent of humanity to its comprehension. To dialogue is to believe that there is no man outside of humanity. For the personalist it is a belief, and if one desires, a faith."[2] Senghor wanted to build bridges between cultures, he wanted to bring Africa into the family of humankind, and give the world a view of its culture and spiritual heritage. He found a spiritual center in *Esprit*. Mounier represented the finest qualities of French philosophical culture, and if Africa would speak in French, it could do no better than to speak through the voice of *Esprit*. It would speak of the person and the community which would seek to find ways and links to others. Personalism opened the way to the idea of humanity that would no longer be an abstract idea but one that lived within man, one that was founded in God. The spirit that poured forth on all humankind exhibited the natural law that bound them to each other. Senghor became the spokesman for a humanity that lived in every culture and hovered over each as a force of union and universality. Each people is called upon to play its unique role in the growing reality of the universe. The Renaissance of our age would be the person, the dignity of man as it had been proclaimed by Pico della Mirandola. If the Renaissance was the rebirth of the person, then it pointed to the mask behind which lived the microcosm of humankind: intellect, will, and practical creativity.

Personalism was a revolt from the false attempts to reduce philosophy to a theory of knowledge; it sought to bring about a community between thinking, acting, and doing. Our contemporary fantasy allows us to separate the person from his writing. It stands in radical contrast to the ancient tradition of student and teacher, of the practical development of intellect and moral action.

---

[2]Ibid., 125.

In a letter of Porphyry (circa 233-305 C.E.) to his wife Marcella, we read words that we have often forgotten. We recall that Porphyry was Plotinus's student and friend, and that it was Porphyry who edited Plotinus's works in six groups of nine which we know as the Enneads. To Marcella, Porphyry wrote: "It is not fitting for a man who is not purified from unholy deeds to speak of God himself, nor must we suppose that he who speaks of Him with such is not guilty of a crime. We should hear and use speech concerning God as though in His presence. Godlike deeds should precede talk of God and in the presence of the multitude we should keep silence concerning Him, for the knowledge of God is not suitable to the vain conceit of the soul. Esteem it better to keep silence than to let fall random words about God."[3] The noble soul approaches the object of philosophy with dignity and respect. Man's life is a preparation for this journey to God and each step along the path should cleanse the soul of its impurities.

We do not assume to bear the vision of Porphyry to the personalists or to Senghor, but we are willing to affirm that the preciousness of the person is closely related to the purity of the soul, and the awe which fills the soul as it bears its way toward God. Human life remains profane without a sense of the majesty and goodness which flow from the divine Oneness. If there were something attractive for Senghor in Mounier's thought, it was this nobility that was given to the person, not simply because of his individuality, but for the divinity that lay masked in him. The philosopher Jules Lachelier (1832-1918), whose thought was close to Mounier's, remarked: "I don't believe in continuous and infallible progress even in the scientific and industrial realm. I believe that everything or almost everything in this realm depends upon the purity and vigor of souls and that if this purity and vigor continue to diminish, we and our descendants will see barbarism again in every form."[4] We speak of progress only if we believe that the quality of man's spiritual life is enhanced and deepened. Otherwise, we face the reality of a coming barbarism that will accompany the vast and startling advances in science and technology. The fact that we can assume the possibility of a value-free human activity is a sign of the new barbarism, what others have seen embodied in the "rebellion of the masses." This rebellion destroys what we believe has always been the dignity of man, that is, the capacity for dialogue, what Senghor calls, in a grander manner, the dialogue of cultures. But the question which will always come forth relates to the meaning and substance of dialogue. Dialogue is the achievement of

---

[3]*Porphyry's Letter to His Wife Marcella concerning the Life Philosophy and the Ascent to the Gods* (Grand Rapids: Phanes Press, 1986), 48-49.
[4]*Le Personnalisme*, 130.

reason. It requires the willingness to be informed, to renounce the pseudomonologue of the man who pretends to be like God, a truth bearer who demands obeisance and conformity, the man who assumes to know what is best for others. Dialogue demands openness and understanding, a sense of the fallibility of man's humanity.

Maurice Blondel (1861-1949) in a letter to his friend Wehrlé said: "Nothing is more essential than the manifestation in our thoughts, in our beings and actions, of that natural and incurable incompleteness or rather, incompletableness [*inachevabilité*]."[5] This incomplete nature of our intelligence and action does not necessarily imply a skepticism. We are not in the either/or situation where we must either accept given truths or find a home in skepticism. We usually like the taste of both, but find either the one or the other indigestible as an exclusive nourishment. We stand in the "between," that is, in dialogue attempting to discover how demanding is our search for truth and how powerful our unconquerable sense of doubt. The plague of doubt leads us closer to our reasonable and prudent character than the confines of truth. Dialogue is not arbitrary conversation or chatter. We turn to dialogue because we are already in dialogue. The emergence of human intelligence is both monologic and dialogic. We talk with ourselves when we prefer the road to wisdom, when we follow either the ways of Heraclitus or that of Parmenides. These men sought wisdom in contemplation. We find dialogue suitable to our intelligence when we raise the question of the meaning of action and discussion. There are human concerns that require continuous discussion. They require temperance and courage, and above all, prudence. We learn to be virtuous in order to be able to deal artfully with political, moral, and intellectual problems which defy definition, in other words, problems which defy factual resolutions. Where the fact or the controlled experiment is not feasible, we need the dialogue.

Truth is a mode of comprehending the world. Moral and intellectual dependence is an awakening of consciousness and conscience. Through this awakening we become profoundly aware of the depths of relationships that draw us to other men and peoples. We discover that in the mutual dependence of man upon man, we find the humanity which we preferred to express in the abstract now lives in experience.

Personalism is always revolutionary and radically threatening to those who have found security in ideology, in a philosophy of history which has dissolved contingency into necessity and freedom into destiny. Personalism is radically dangerous to a collectivist materialism and to an egocentricism that seeks the pleasures of sensuality. Personalism finds the reality in virtue, and in the sanctity of the creative

---

[5]Ibid., 90.

act. It demands that man look behind the self that hides the person. Man seeks what has been an eternal inheritance. If we assume that man is not only an animal in search of a meaning, but a possessor, a domicile of a divine spirit, then we understand why every age seeks to find the meaning of the person. Every search is different, attempting to discover and unveil an unfathomable gift which never yields to comprehension, and rightfully flees definition. The search has not only its own logic, but its own poetry. It finds its dialogue, but also its images. Its conversation is subtle and changing, but the images remain permanent in their evolution.

The visions of the biblical Prophets are divinely inspired and their imagery returns to us again and again. We speak of it with new terms and phrases, but the images remain the same in grandeur and beauty. Dialogue is possible only where we have imagery, where the dream accompanies the immediacies of concrete reality. We look to poetry for words that have become signs and symbols. Poetry yields a realm of dreams. This realm gives us the possibility for spiritual dialogue.

Lachelier reminded us that "the person welcomes the conflicts which tear at him and push him forward. He accepts all of external nature without which he would not be conscious of himself. He is open to the supernatural which enlightens without destroying him. The person is not an individual shriveled up in himself, satisfying only himself. He is this contradictory and unfulfilled being who understands the necessity for being attentive to everything by giving himself to everything in order to perfect and realize himself in a true communion."[6] This person is consciousness and conscience. Through them he relates to nature and humankind. He finds community and spiritual communion. Communion requires conversation that is always threatened with the silence of violence. The word must stretch the reality of its spirit upon the realm of perception, and through the word, this perceptive world learns to speak. We call the word dialogue or conversation. The word is a work of art that is cultivated in consciousness and conscience. Man becomes the creator of forms through the manifestation of the word. With the word, he forms the imagery of the intellect and the will. In the word, he discovers his dialogic partners, the source of other worlds of thought and dreams. He also unveils the hidden possibilities of his own person, realms of reality which he never imagined. In the conversation, man reveals to himself, and to the other, new realms of being. Here begin the marvels of revelation, those unexpected and unknown regions of reality which we touch through others. There is futility in self-contemplation; the self seems to find only the image for conversation.

---

[6]Ibid., 130.

Self-contemplation can begin only with the divine light which strives to fill the soul and open those moments of silence which have become enamored with self in idolic contemplation.

At the end of his autobiography Senghor stated: "It is time to conclude my *What I Believe.* I will do it with a word, affirming my faith in the *Civilization of the Universal* to which I dedicate the few years that are left me in this life."[7] This universality belongs to the dialogue among peoples lost in the history of humankind, lost through separation, conquest, and exploitation. The poet yearns for its renewal, for the power of the word to bring again the message of Plato's idea of purifying love: the ascent of the soul from sensuality to spirituality. This spirituality hovers melancholically over all creation, seeking to find a dwelling where there is violence, disorder, and anarchy, seeking beauty where there is ugliness, goodness where there is evil. Senghor, who read the classics, now in his old age belongs to the world of the philosopher, the man of wisdom. He understands Plato's words that "those who go uninitiated and unsanctified to the other world, will lie in the mire, but he who arrives there initiated and purified, will dwell with the gods.... And I in my life have, so far as I could, left nothing undone, and have striven in every way to make myself one of them [the mystics]. But whether I have striven aright and have met with success, I believe I shall know clearly when I have arrived there, very soon, if it is God's will."[8]

Men dialogue because they have ideas to discuss with each other. Socrates explained his belief in the eternity of the soul to Cebes and Simmias. We discuss the same enduring problems from the perspective of our age. We look with wonder on those figures who, like Socrates, voice their ideas in poetry and conversation. We hear Senghor speak to us through his images and dreams and we dialogue with him. His presence arouses in us that consciousness and conscience which make us partners in a world that needs the voices that speak in imagery and show us the ways of the imagination.

Mounier began his study of dialogue in his *Traité du caractère* with a remark that indicated the direction which his philosophy persistently followed. "More than any other personal activity," he said, "the intelligence can neither be defined nor exercised in isolation. When it excessively turns upon itself, it soon wanders toward a closed and autistic world. The fate of every thought is inebriated by its own self-sufficiency, and flees confrontation, becomes enervated, and slides into reverie, there to harden and turn toward the fixed idea, becoming

---

[7]*Ce que je crois*, 231.
[8]*Phaedo*, trans. H.N. Fowler (London: William Heinemann, 1947), 69 D-E.

obscure and overcast."[9] In these few lines, Mounier has shown us the dangers of intellectual isolation. He reveals to us the violence that is ever present in human thinking: the movement toward the closed realm of being. Only at that moment when man finds no converse with his fellow does he realize that he has become either fool or wise man. The reasonable human condition is dialogic. Its natural condition is the absence of dialogue. It is violence. This violence is not an external condition which can be arbitrarily removed and set aside, it is the reality of man's nature, the force that constitutes his intelligence. It is its negative reality, a moment of its essence. If this force is absent, man loses his character. Where it is limited, man returns to a natural animality. Violence and reason are conflicting realities forming the human substance, its distinctive nature.

When Senghor was invited in 1984 to become a member of the world's most prestigious academy, the Académie française, it was his friend and political colleague Edgar Faure who spoke in his behalf. He mentioned that "you [Senghor] are a law of humanism incarnated among men. Your law is the gravitation toward the Universal.... What is admirable about your law is that it addresses all beliefs and even that belief which is searching. It reveals the riches of man rather than abolishing differences. It sees the condition of its achievement in giving and receiving. In this, you show the way to a symbiosis of the Universal among the religious allegiances and notably to a syndetic approach between Christianity and Islam. The latter can lead to the alleviation of grave misunderstandings, to averting heavy and pressing dangers, and to the preparation of a response to the highest exigencies of our spirituality. In this way, your universal civilization is not only theory, it is the announcement, it is the offering to youth, to all youths."[10]

Edgar Faure did not only describe a figure seated on a throne, he showed a man of dialogue who reached out to humankind, asking it to speak and share the spiritual heritage which the divine inspired in different forms and figures of the people of the universe. Senghor felt that it should be a poet of Africa who should add his voice following in the spiritual paths of those great biblical Prophets calling forth to humankind to share in the love, the goodness God gave to his creation. Senghor knows that this capacity to share is embodied in the capacity for dialogue. With Mounier he felt a companionship which gave him the courage and strength to struggle for that dialogue of cultures that has always been precious to him.

---

[9]*Traité du caractère* (Paris: Editions du Seuil, 1974), 327.
[10]Discours de remerciement et de réception à l'Académie française (Paris: Editions du Seuil, 1984), 92, 94-5.

Dialogue and monologue seem to be the alternatives that face the human situation. Nothing expresses the monologic situation more fully than the answer Moses received from God when he posed the question: "Who am I that I should go to Pharaoh and free the Israelites from Egypt?" God told Moses that he would be with him but Moses asked another question: "When I come to the Israelites and say to them the God of your fathers has sent me and they ask me, What is His name, what shall I say to them? And God said to Moses, *Ehyeh-Asher-Ehyeh* [I Am That I Am, I Am Who I Am, I Will Be What I Will Be]. He continued, thus shall you say to the Israelites, Ehyeh sent me to you."[11] In these words are the source of the monologue, the reality of man's listening. His capacity to hear slowly commands the vision of the world. Moses hears the words and he does the will of God, but God can say nothing more about his reality than what can be found in the identity of Being: I Am and I Will Be because I Have Always Been. Here there is no unknown, undefined, and arbitrary moment. Two words form the awesome efficacy of God: "I Am," but in this sense the "I Am" is not abstract, it belongs to history acting through its presence in human events, in man's thought and will. The last remark of God to Moses is fundamental: "Thus shall you speak to the Israelites: The Lord, the God of your fathers, the God of Abraham, the God of Isaac and the God of Jacob has sent me to you. This shall be my name forever. This my appellation for all eternity."[12] To *Ehyeh* man writes poetry, for *Ehyeh* he fights wars, and in obedience to *Ehyeh* he seeks to live in the way of the Law and the way of love.

Moses was "slow of speech and slow of tongue," hardly a candidate for the art of speaking, for the rhetoricians and sophists, men who seek ways and manners to conduct reasonable discourses in community life, who investigate the limits of human knowledge, who find the qualities of the good decisions and the prudent consensus. Here we discover the art of dialogue, that precious conversation of reason which recognizes no higher power than its own effectiveness. This is the art of conviction which bears in it the capacity to dominate through the reasonable. In this realm of the reasonable, the conversation dominates over the logical conflict of opposites. The conversation is not bound by theory. It uses the subtleties of human confrontation: shades of voice, facial expressions, humor, irony. These are the realities that move men toward conviction and show at the same time. The fact is that in human discourse, as in knowledge, there are no absolutes. The art of conversation is rooted in the willingness to speak and be spoken to, to hear and see what has

[11]Exod. 3:13.
[12]Ibid.

previously not been seen or heard. In the absence of God there is prudent dialogue. This is the humanism of the word which calls out to all men for a meaningful exchange of opinions. To God's word Moses responds in faith. There can be only poetical debates with God, terrifying cries of abandonment and incomprehensibility, but finally there is only the divine truth and it alone is truth. We cannot think of Socrates before the blazing bush, hiding his face because he feared to look at God. Socrates knew the wonders of human knowledge, he comprehended the multiple forms of the human psyche. He could not live away from the marketplace, from that search for the dimensions of human life which he considered precious and absolute.

We leave Moses and Socrates to their experiences of truths. In a distinct way we know that their opposition belongs to our thinking, determining our way of life and the values which guide it. Mounier noted that "the first moment of dialogue is that of *opposition.* It is in the latter that thought becomes conscious of its limits and aspirations. We encounter it at each crisis in the growth of personality. It is the form of adolescent thought. Every great discovery of thought, Bergson said, begins with a 'no.' In spite of appearance this 'no' already guides the affirmations which come forth as the plant from the seed. You need no experience of the dialectic of discovery to criticize twenty-year-old boys for the 'negative' character of their first acts of awareness."[13] Dialogue is not natural to life; it is not synonymous with it but is cultivated and nurtured in it. Human relationships become civilized; they are not naturally prudent or temperate. Dialogue is a supreme human achievement, the realization of a reason that has always contested with a life process formed in aggression, the will to power. Personalism is an attempt to reaffirm the humanity that lives in man and that must be awakened in every age to its responsibilities and grandeur. Mounier spoke of youth because he knew that during it the dialogic process was rare and seemed to be dampened by the energies aroused by concrete values and positive achievement. The struggle for survival is dominant. Opposition exists to be crushed rather than comprehended and acted upon. However we think of youth, we are aware that in it lies oppositions in the depths of radical separation. They are dealt with through either excessive passivity or the furor of physical conflict. Slowly we realize that in living thought opposition does not exist in an isolated state but, as Mounier noted, "only in relationship with an *actual and emerging affirmation.* A concrete thought is formed by two confronting

---

[13]*Traité du caractère*, 329-30.

ideas in a supple antithesis radically different from the 'all or nothing' of fixed and hardened thought."[14]

In the realization that the exploration of truth is a collective enterprise, we become conscious that what we call humankind is a community in search of its multiple and varied reality. Man cries out to his fellowman: Where are you? The question reflects the one we heard through the centuries when we remember the voice of God calling to Adam, "Where are you?" These three words have become the source of imagery. We hear this voice in our consciousness and conscience. We know that it is not only our physical presence but our spiritual reality that is needed. If we can imagine that God called to Adam and the latter replied: "I heard the sound of you in the garden, and I was afraid because I was naked so I hid" (Gen. 3:9), then we understand that dialogue between the calling and the hiding, a dialogue which assumes infinite forms in imagery. Adam and Eve had eaten of the tree of the knowledge of good and evil and both became aware of their nakedness. They delighted in the idea of being like divine beings who know. Driven into the confines of human knowledge, unable to answer the divine call, man is separated both from God and the inadequacies of knowledge. But man wonders if he has not found both a blessing and a curse. In God, man does not discover the ways of knowledge. In knowledge man finds that he is denied a lost truth, but has the responsibility of asking the question of meaning: What does it mean to have lost the possibility of being like divine beings who know good and evil? Man has no answer but many possibilities. These make it necessary for him to search for his fellowman, to speak with him, to share knowledge, to declare an interdependence from which the human community arises. If there is the improbable possibility that God called to Adam in need, there is the possibility that we call to each from need and dependence.

Whatever personalism tells us, we know that it speaks to our dependence in dialogue and community. We know that we are dependent upon the word that convinces and persuades. The word can imprison or liberate us. It is the tool either of those who seek to imitate divine beings, or of those who seek the dialogue of cultures. We can imagine like Valéry that "we are shut up *outside* ourselves." The word remains in defiance of every political and moral incarceration.

Mounier said that "the love of truth is diffusive in itself. A nonmissionary faith is a dead faith. The need for proof, for collective assent are the elementary components of thought. In this passion for communication we find the double movement of thought: availability and affirmation. The effort for communication works ceaselessly for

[14]Ibid., 330.

forms of expression and deprives spontaneous thought of false ideas and utopias."[15] Even in communication there lies a threat to the person. Communication seeks to convince but also to conquer the spirit of the other. Where there is no friendship, there can be no dialogue; where there is not assumption of belief, attachment to an idea, there is only debate for advantage or self-pride. Words become arbitrary tools of intellectual duels. Communication can never be separated from the search for power. Only the poet-philosopher speaks of dialogue as a pure spiritual act, a product of the intellect.

In his last book, *Personalism* (1950), Mounier quoted from an article he wrote in *Esprit* (February 1933) called "Eloge de la force" (Praise of Force). In this article, he stated: "Love is a struggle; life is a struggle against death; spiritual life is a struggle against the inertia of matter and the sloth of the body. The person attains self-consciousness not through ecstasy but by force of mortal combat; and force is one of its attributes.... A person comes to full maturity only at the moment when he is seized of loyalties he values more than life itself.... There is no society, order, or right which does not originate in struggle between forces, or is not sustained by some force."[16] It is not difficult to imagine Senghor finding in these words ideas that would free him for the combat against materialism, eudaemonism, and skepticism. We can never liberate ourselves from the search for meaning, from hearing the call to our being. Before it is destroyed and we become the tools of necessity and self-indulgence, the question of meaning and purpose exercises a powerful influence upon us. We cannot avoid the struggle that accompanies our desire to find some way to answer the question of meaning. Driven from paradise, we face the havoc into which we were driven. Our task has been to establish new orders without the divine knowledge of good and evil. We discover the human condition and give it whatever description seems suitable to our experience. But we are constantly aware that the individual must become the person, that the family is the base of civil society and the state a reflection of the values of the latter. Mounier reminded us that it is in the human struggle for the person that we become human. In that movement from the individual to the person, we discover the meaning of family and society, we realize the capacity to hear and comprehend with others.

Listening becomes the essential element of the human conversation, whether it is with the fellowman or with the divine. I am reminded of those fascinating words of the Prophet Micah: "He has told you O Man what is good, and what the Lord requires of you: Only to do justice and

---

[15]Ibid., 331.

[16]*Personalism* (Notre Dame: University of Notre Dame Press, 1952), 49-50.

to love goodness, And to walk modestly with your God, Then will your name achieve wisdom" (Mic. 6:8-9). We listen to these words. They cast a moral command over life. We are responsible for the violence which dwells in our life, which turns us against each other and fills us with remorse and bewilderment. God's call is to both conscience and consciousness. It awakens us from our destitute individuality and it makes us realize that to become a person is to know that we are bound in human relationships, to a morality which we have constructed, but not inspired. This morality was present in our being from the time of its creation; it is synonymous with self-realization. This is the natural law of creation. The divine command breaks into our lives and sends forth a radical upheaval which separates the good from the bad, the violence of daily life from reason, rationality from its moral constructs. Life, as Mounier stated, is conflict, but this conflict is not only physical. More fundamentally it is spiritual. It bears in itself the violence of blindness rooted in jealousy. From the story of Cain and Abel, we listen to a tale of fraternal rivalry and envy. "The Lord paid heed to Abel and his offering but to Cain and his offering, he paid no heed. Cain was much distressed and his face fell. And the Lord said to Cain, Why are you distressed, And why is your face fallen? Surely, if you do right, There is uplift" (Gen. 4:4-7). The remainder of the tale is known, but for us it is the story of fratricide, the beginning of human history with its despairing cry for divine light, for the powers of reason to hold in check the voice of seduction, the unending chaos that lives in the violence of lost paradise.

Personalism is an appeal to man's conscience. It asks him to struggle against the immorality and injustice he finds in the world, to raise the voice of that moral substance that was his from the creation. It asks him to see and hear the reality of the world around him, to know that there is no escape into the divine or into an egocentric indifference without the loss of personality. "Experience demonstrates," said Mounier, "that there is no value that is not born of conflict or established without struggle, from political order to social justice, from sexual love to human unity or, for Christians, to the Kingdom of God. Violence must be condemned, but to evade it at any cost, is to renounce all the principal tasks of mankind."[17] Mounier revealed a fundamental truth of man's moral and intellectual existence. He showed that the rule of violence is indispensable for intellectual and moral life. The punishment of Cain is borne by humankind. We face this judgment with courage and prudence. "You shall become a ceaseless wanderer on earth," this is our moral and intellectual destiny, the eternal struggle against disorder and violence. But there is a dignity and strength in the ever-present conflict that is

---

[17]Ibid., 71.

human life. We must struggle for every moral, aesthetic, and intellectual achievement. The divine is silent. In this silence, we fight to reveal what lies behind the mask of our individuality. We have lost the capacity to be like the divine beings. We have not lost the ability to uncover the nobility of man's fight for moral dignity and intellectual innovation.

Mounier made it clear to those who believe in the capacity of redeeming the creation that "to desire life at all costs is, some day, to buy life at the price of all reason for living. We have no authentic existence until we have an interior stronghold of values or of devotion, against which we do not believe that the fear of death itself could prevail."[18] Violence deprives the inner self of its beliefs in justice and goodness, of its strength to resist the demands of immediate pleasures, the accumulation of wealth and the inordinate desire for power over man and nation. The dialogue of human existence calls forth to those who share with us the need for the moral perspective, for the freedom of intellectual and artistic work. Here we grasp the meaning of Senghor's work, his desire to reach out to the peoples of the world and talk to them again of universality, humanism, and spiritual evolution. He knows that these words may be empty sounds that reveal the hopelessness that can lie in the concreteness of the human situation. He also knows that they are meaningful symbols which every age must seek to express. We cannot live without the right to dream, to conjure up images of the lost paradise which will always be ours. Even if we are the children of fratricide, we cannot avoid the fact that we are persons through conscience.

What the philosopher, poet, or the artist enunciated in words, sounds, or colors is significant. We understand the reality of our existence only in confrontation with political and moral situations demanding decision and sacrifice. In action, we assume, our words find the incarnation that gives them their meaning. In action we discover those mysterious links between courage and prudence and the decision to act, to say yes or no to a course of action, to assume the responsibility for what we do or refuse to do. If action is part of the logic of thinking, it remains deeply tied to the moral and intellectual attitude in and through which we conduct our lives. Action allows us to fulfill the obligation to the values we have accepted and which have become our beliefs. We know that we struggle for these beliefs and maintain them only through the willingness to suffer for them. "Culture," Mounier stated, "does not exist in any of its domains, in the heaping-up of knowledge, but in a deep transformation of the subject, enabling him to fulfill ever new possibilities in response to ever new renewed calls from within. As

[18]Ibid., 71-72.

someone has said, culture is that which remains when one no longer knows anything – it is what the man himself has become."[19] It is what we have become that will determine when and where we will act. This applies not only to man, but to nations. We expect much of those nations that have given the world remarkable statements of universality, of human rights, and a recognition of natural law, but expectations often live far beyond reality. We live with disappointment and with despair. In his defiance of the dichotomy between expectation and existence, man creates conscience. In conscience man finds in himself an awareness of the Cain-Abel conflict. Man wanders upon the earth with a spirit condemned to struggle which he will never conquer without destroying himself.

From personalism, Senghor draws moral and spiritual inspiration, confirming his faith in man's spiritual destiny and the dialogue of cultures which is essential to his conception of the world. This movement, which he discovered in the 1930s, was both religious and humanistic. It represented what he believed to be the finest tradition of French culture, which had its roots in Montaigne, Bayle, Molière. Senghor knew however, that traditions make wonderful subjects for books, plays, and poetry, but when they remain without realization in human behavior, in political and moral decisions, they lose their force and vitality. We don't have to be taught the virtues of universal dialogue, we need to learn how to make it a way of life. We need to know that dialogue is not universally applicable. If we demand that it apply where there is no will for it, we increase the violence that threatens the human community. We create the lie. Dialogue is not necessarily applicable for the alleviation of conflict. Violence doesn't naturally yield to it. Violence remains an integral part of dialogue. Reason needs force to hold it in check. Senghor spoke of the need for justice with the words of the spirit. He reminded us that "to wish justice for *others*, is to think with the thought of others in order to be identified with them. This is an efficacious means of reciprocal knowledge. The wars of cultures provoke economic wars which in turn, provoke wars of human self-destruction."[20]

In personalism, Senghor found the belief that the person not only exists, but bears within him transcendence. Culture is a living community of persons which, as Mounier stated, "loses of the universal [as] it begins to dry up into specialism. As soon as it confuses universality with a static notion of totality, it hardens into a system."[21]

---

[19]Ibid., 118-19.
[20]"Pour un humanisme de la francophone," in *Liberté* 3:552.
[21]*Personalism*, 119.

The voice of Senghor reaches us today like sounds in the desert. Humankind searches for the roots with conflict, opposition, and demands for self-determinism. Every people, language, and heritage stakes a claim for independence, seeking to redeem a part of its oppression. History justifies everything. Through the world runs this hysteria of exaggerated national pride with few voices still speaking of universality and humanism. God has been sequestered by every national entity.

Senghor is the lonely poet of international cooperation. He stands alone like the prophet and speaks words that men do not want to hear. He paints images they do not allow themselves to see, but he is there in this blindness to be heard and seen. Within him there is the primeval dialogue. He is Samuel listening. We want to understand this fascinating man from Senegal who speaks French, who believes that Montesquieu and the Abbé Grègoire have set forth for us the mission of universalism which he, Senghor, has continued through his love of not only Africa and France, but of humanity. We can say that Senghor's word is now silent, that his message, like the imperial message of the emperor in Kafka's painfully beautiful fable, will never be given to humankind. The message is always on the way, but always "away from here." Never will it be heard in the world. When Joseph came to his brothers, they exclaimed with scorn: "Here comes the dreamer." Hopefully our poet, meeting such scorn, will, like the phoenix, arise in a new court where his dreams and images will reveal a reality which will convince men to follow reason and justice. The realm of dialogue has only just begun its history. From the ashes of violence, reason, like the emerging plant, shows its bowed but forceful head. Senghor cultivates the creative possibilities of the human spirit. We look upon him with wonder and joy. In him there is life and beauty. There is devastating sadness.

8

Senghor Encounters Jacques Maritain

If Emmanuel Mounier is no longer well known, the same cannot be said of Jacques Maritain (1882-1973). His name takes us into a world where the divine and the human belong to each other and have formed a temporal and spiritual architecture. We are living in a universe created and redeemed by God. The divine-human drama is molded by the skill and beauty of one of its finest interpreters and artists: St. Thomas Aquinas, the composer and master of the *Summa Theologiae.* It was from this vast compendium of knowledge that Maritain drew inspiration and strength. He belongs to a world in which truth is enunciated by the Church and has been interpreted through the ages by its theologians, poets, sculptors, architects, and painters. This is a realm of being in which man finds not only a faith but a vast realm of possibilities for the elaboration of this faith. Here the word is given, but its manner and modes of expression lies open and undetermined. Man is part of a creation that is not his own. He is subject to the divine powers that have been in him from eternity. He stands under God's law, as its servant and enunciator. Man's reason is his way to God. Reason distinguishes man from all other beings. It makes him aware of his limits and his possibilities. He is responsible for knowledge. He is obliged to know not only the principles of his faith, but as St. Thomas stated, "the general principles of right and wrong; [while] each man is obliged to know the duties of his state in life."[1]

Senghor found deep kinship with Maritain, similar to the companionship he found with Claudel, Teilhard, and Mounier. Senghor sought a philosophy and a theory of the arts that preserved the sanctity of the divine and the uniqueness of man. Nothing was more precious to him than poetic creativity, but even this creativity could seek only to

---

[1]*Summa Theologiae* (Blackfriars), Question 76, The cause of sin from the reason, article 2, is ignorance sinful? (London: Eyre & Spotteswoode, 1969).

approach the divine, never to be the divine. More often men forget this distinction and seek to find in themselves the divinity they envy in God. Philosophic life is the attempt to find the capacities of reason, knowing that there are limits which we do not determine but which are determined for us. In these limits lies the reality of the unknown and unknowable, a reality that we know belongs to all realms of being. We know God in our reason, but we know that this reason is finite, and through this finiteness God's ways are shown to man.

In 1970, in his article "La Grande Vallée fertile" (The Great Fertile Valley), Senghor spoke of man's relationship to nature, the source of imagery and poetry. This relationship became and has remained a dialogue. He mentioned Jacques Maritain who remarked that "this intercommunication between the inner being of things and the inner being of the human self is a mode of divination." Commenting on Maritain's words, Senghor said: "There is no opposition between subject and object, the artist and nature, in fact, there is no opposition between inner and exterior reality. Man is not content to dissect things with the intelligence of his glance. He is touched, moved [*ému*] by the waves which deep being sends forth from the center of the *Other*, and this depth awakens in him emotions which he expresses in a work of art. The latter provokes in other men the same emotion, and the same imagery reaction which is at the same time sensual and spiritual."[2]

This intercommunication is a fundamental insight into man's relationship to being, to both nature and his fellowman. Here we come to that startling and pleasant realization that what we perceive is only the shell of an existence. We are within a creation whose beings have depths of existence which we are only beginning to comprehend. The divine creation has left us with realities which are just beginning to be explored, which have much to yield to us. Our communication with nature and self seeks either to fathom the depths of the self or to transform the divine into human form. Since man has never forgotten his longing for divinity, these anthropomorphic forms dominate his art and his science. Man also searches for the divine anthropocentrically, that is, he seeks within the self to bring forth from the profundity of his being the infinite of his reality, the divinity which he believes is the source of his being. The search for a humanism which brings together these realms of being is an "integral humanism." Senghor believed that in Maritain's thought and, in particular, in his book *Integral Humanism* (1936), he found the humanism that he longed for. But apart from this title, which Senghor found appealing, it was Maritain's writings on art and poetry, which revealed the essence of humanism. It was in 1927, after Senghor had

---

[2]*Liberté* 3:253.

arrived in Paris, that Maritain published his beautiful text *The Frontiers of Poetry* (1927). The madness that embraces man's atheism, and the violence that overwhelms his emotive drive to find anthropormorphic forms for his stormy adventures into the heavens, could end only in passionate exhaustion, and bewilderment, that is, in spiritual death.

If, for a moment, we turn from man's search for self-deification, and return to the belief that the world was created and that there is a creator, man's place in the universe becomes profoundly different. In no human activity is the longing for self-sufficiency more dominant than in the creative arts. Here we don't need to recognize the heroism of Prometheus. The "fire" which is the source of creativity has been man's eternally, a natural condition shared with the gods, but not necessarily taken from them. Maritain noted in the beginning of his discussion of the arts in his book *The Frontiers of Poetry*, that "God's ideas are not like our concepts, that is, representative signs drawn from things, intended to introduce into a creative mind the immensity of that which is, and to render this mind, consonant with existents (actual or possible), independent of it. God's ideas precede things, they create them."[3]

The foundation for Maritain's discussion of the artist and the arts lay in these words. They establish the priority of God's reality and the work of creation. God's presence permeates reality. Man's powers lie in his receptivity, his capacity to receive the formative ideas that lie in creation, to grasp them as the source of the beauty. We are beings whose thoughts are not formed by what we perceive, but by what controls and dominates our perception. Perception is possible because it masks a spiritual force which faintly reveals itself in perception. What we see and hear is only the beginning, the starting point of a journey into realms of a higher reality for which we cultivate our reason and feeling. We search to comprehend the nature of the idea, a power that "does not render the mind consonant with the real, [but] renders the real consonant with the mind."[4]

We find these words difficult to comprehend. They offer us that either/or situation which seems to defy the nature of life. The mind is rarely consonant with what it knows. It is always beyond the reality it embraces. What it knows remains dependent upon the mind's formative capacities. When these decline, and there is an identification between the mind and its object, the former has declined and lost its essence. It is obvious to us that the formative powers of the mind draw the real to it and form it into an image. Here lies the essence of the creative act, the

---

[3]*Art and Scholasticism and The Frontiers of Poetry* (Notre Dame: University of Notre Dame, 1974), 120.
[4]Ibid., 121.

formative power of the image, the realization that to know is beyond identification and classification. Knowledge is creative in its capacity to give renewed form to what it is potentially capable of receiving. We stand between the actuality of identification and the pleasures of formative articulation. The mind in its strength and weakness moves from one reality to another. We are fascinated by our creative powers, but we recognize their frailty and fallibility. We find our humanity in a metaphysical uncertainty which establishes the finite quality of human existence. Man is a being who is always in search of knowing, never certain of its permanency and persistence. Here the artist, poet, and scientist discover the glory of work, but also that dependence upon divine grace which gives them the force to carry on their activity. Lying within this force is the painful despair that this activity is borrowed, and we are always thankful. We are rarely masters of our fate. How much wiser we are when we recognize how profound are the depths of the unknown surrounding our life.

In the profundity of his idealism, Senghor experienced the faith of uncertainty. We always wonder at the strength of a faith that was, throughout his life, so deeply challenged by political and moral disappointment and betrayal. The uncertainty which battles and storms at the human situation causes it to despair and rail against life, to defy life and grow in determination and conviction. In speaking of Maritain's integral humanism, Senghor stated that "we must first comprehend the whole planet, with its five continents, its different races and civilizations. It is possible that after the soldiers, the settlers, and the missionaries, the French university will, in its turn, explore the continents and the civilization, and extract from them the 'substantive marrow.' When all these forces are harmoniously gathered and mixed, we can elaborate on integral humanism."[5]

The reality of this idea of humanism has no correspondence with existence. In fact, what we observe contradicts the idea of a new form of human existence dependent upon the vision of the oneness of mankind. The contradictions are not mutually cooperative parts, but profoundly antagonistic and combative. Yet, there is that hope which emerges from the needs of reason to speak in universal terms, to imagine the domination of the spirit over matter, to find in the individual a propensity to reason. But this propensity is faint and limpid; it yearns for substance and finds it only in the faith of reason, in the community of those for whom this rational faith is meaningful and effective. We find hope in the faith that tells us that in *that day* God and his world will again find harmony. The faith of reason becomes a poetry of faith, a dream

---

[5]"De la Francité – à la Négritude," in *Liberté* 3:550.

which excites the imagination and creates images, and various forms of rhythms and forms.

Maritain realized that art and the artist allowed man to imagine a closeness to the divine which at times touched the demonic. Nowhere else was the experience of creativity more deeply felt and enjoyed than in the creative act. Valéry's writings on Leonardo da Vinci reflected this unlimited esteem for the powers of the mind. "I propose," Valéry said in his essay on the method of Leonardo, "to imagine a man whose activities are so diverse that if I postulate a ruling idea behind them all, there could be none more universal. And I want this man to possess an infinitely keen perception of the difference of things, the adventures of which perception might well be called analysis. I see him as aiming at all things; he is always thinking in terms of the universe and of vigor [Hostinato rigore, obstinate rigor – Leonardo's motto].... He leaves behind him churches and fortresses; he fashions ornaments instinct with gentleness and grandeur, besides a thousand mechanical devices and the rigorous calculations of many a research."[6]

The longing for artistic perfection is natural to man. Man, the poet, the painter, the scientist, seeks to explore the infinite ways of the intellect which remain a mystery to him. The search for the subtleties of the thinking *I* offers man an indescribable fascination. Man is driven by a demon which refuses to allow him to remain within fixed limitations or defined aptitudes. Man belongs to a species which is always on a journey in the search for truth. The experience of the poet lies with the magic and mystery of the word. The experience of the writer is with the word that is profoundly individual and unique. It is an experience he can give to no other. The word comes from one language into another. It finds in each a unique home. It can be read. It can bring joy and excitement. It can open to us a way into the writer's experience. This experience we can only faintly share with another. We describe it with intimacy and emotion. In it lies the artistic wonder which brings together what is human and what touches man from other realms of reality. Here man experiences forms of art that live not only from their presence, but from the life and death struggle in which they live and in which they die. "The poem," Valéry remarked, "does not die for having lived; it is expressly designed to be born again from its ashes and to become endlessly what it has just been. Poetry can be recognized by its property, that it tends to get itself

[6]"Introduction to the Method of Leonardo Da Vinci," in *Leonardo, Poe, Mallarmé* (Princeton: Princeton University Press, 1972), 5-6.

reproduced in its own form: it stimulates us to reconstruct it identically."[7]

The fact that art has a life of its own caused dismay for Maritain. He saw in it a demonic exaggeration of the human work, the temptation of the serpent handing to man that enticing promise: You shall be as the divine beings. This temptation hounds man's creativity; it draws him toward a sweetness that is hard to resist. Man is led to believe that there can be a harmony that would erase the knowledge of the difference between the divine and the human. In pure beauty, this harmony is reestablished. We journey toward this purity attempting to set aside the cavernous gap that held man apart from the divine, that is never truly his. It is difficult to elaborate Senghor's attitude toward this conflict which seeks to measure the limits of man's potentiality. But there is in Senghor a wondrous optimism about man and the future of humankind. We imagine this lonely man of faith speaking words of universality, chanting the depths of man's poetic uniqueness and showing us the way to that universal dialogue of cultures upon which we all depend for the spiritual progress of the universe. From this hope and its visions, there is this deepening confidence in the presence of God, the growing awareness of the consequence of God's existence, his drawing us forth from our spiritual potentiality. Divinity hovers about us, preserving us from the pessimism of moral and political despair, giving us the courage to transform reality and to stand with enchantment before endless imagery which is possible for the human soul. Man and his work is like the phoenix dying and living with the forces of despair and regeneration. The dialectic of the struggle is constant, but not repetitive. It is a renewal of life forces developing and enhancing endlessly the human situation.

Maritain was uneasy about the poet's attempt to search for purity. In other words, he looked with fright upon Mallarmé's search to find a pure poetry, a symmetry between word and image. He remarked that "to command our art *to be* art in the pure state, by freeing itself in effect from all conditions of existence in the human subject, is to wish it to usurp for itself the aseity of God."[8] Maritain was haunted by the ongoing struggle of French poets, from Rimbaud to Valéry, to find in poetic reverie a new form of prayer and sanctity. Man believed he had found a new way to enter the lost paradise and to become like the divine Being, which he previously had been denied.

The thoughts and feelings of Maritain concerning art and poetry were realized in his beautiful book *Creative Intuition in Art and Poetry*

---

[7]"Poetry and Abstract Thought," in *The Art of Poetry* (New York: Pantheon Books, 1958), 72.
[8]*The Frontiers of Poetry*, 122.

(1953) when he revealed the nature of the radical conflict between the poets of the second half of the nineteenth and the early twentieth century and the thinkers of the Middle Ages. Speaking of Baudelaire, he noted: "He knew that beauty is one of the Divine Names. But the fact with which his own experience was obsessed and which his extraordinary power of perception made clear – and this event has a crucial significance for poetry in modern times – is that now this Divine Name is detached from God and *reigns separate* in our human heaven. Where Thomas Aquinas had said: 'The existence of all things derives from God's beauty,' Baudelaire says: *Que tu viennes du ciel ou de l'enfer, qui importe* – whether beauty comes from heaven or hell what do we care? It is always beauty; and the devil is still beautiful."[9]

This last question reveals the differences that always emerge when a divine name is detached from God and given a human face. These differences show a profound and radical chasm separating those who believe that the creation is beautiful and man must bring forth this beauty, and those who are convinced that they are creators whose task is to give the world the reality of their creative act. If the world is beautiful in and through creation, it is beautiful because of divine creation, but if it is beautiful because we impose this quality upon it, then what is significant is no longer the beautiful per se, but man's creative act. We know that through the centuries man has sought to regain not only a cocreatorship with the divine, but to emerge as the unique and unchallenged creator of the world. Man no longer needs divine assistance. He discovers within himself a divinity that is autonomous and self-sufficient. Valéry had noted in this respect that "thought is, in short, the activity which causes what does not exist to come alive in us, lending to it, whether we will or not, our present powers, making us take the part for the whole, the image for reality and giving us the illusion of seeing, acting, suffering and possessing independently of our dear old body, which we leave with the cigarette in an armchair until we suddenly retrieve it when the telephone rings or, no less strongly, when our stomach demands provender."[10]

At times, it appears that the choice between man's devotion to God, and his noble evaluation of the self, offers two irreconcilable positions. But, in fact, it does not. Senghor, who is deeply attached to human dignity and creativity, is moved by passion and an extraordinary trust in the spiritual growth both of man and the universe. This confidence and hope is the wonder of his life. We find the strength for our own optimism

---

[9]*Creative Intuition in Art and Poetry* (Princeton: Princeton University Press, 1977), 177.
[10]"Poetry and Abstract Thought," 73.

and willingness to go forward through this unshakable trust in God. He suffered personally more than most men, challenged God, but believed in him. The God who brought him suffering also ennobled him. In him he found pain but also comfort. The choice was never an abandonment, a surrender, or a self-deification. Man never lost his greatness, but has only forgotten how to testify to it. The poet witnessed the divine presence in the mystery and marvel of the word. The love for the spiritual gifts that create man's uniqueness never allowed Senghor to worship his works. He was a man in whom there was no self-deification, but only an unending search for man's beauty and goodness.

We feel the depths of Senghor's attitude toward man's creative power when we listen to the words he employed to describe the great artists of his time. We mentioned how eager Senghor was to bring to Dakar the great painters. He brought the work of Pablo Picasso, of Marc Chagall, and in 1974 he arranged for an exhibition of the work of Pierre Soulages. In an article "The Creative Power of Pierre Soulages," Senghor spoke of the work of a painter who was also a poet. In his introductory words, he said: "If we chose Pierre Soulages, it is because after the generation of Picasso and Chagall, Soulages is one of the greatest painters of the second half of the twentieth century. His work is the highest expression of pure painting, and like his two predecessors, it is significant for the lessons he can give our young painters. We never had the intention of enclosing them in a black cultural ghetto. If they allow themselves to be influenced, we wish that this be through artists whose art has affinity with black art."[11]

If again we hear in Senghor's words the relationship between particularity and universality, we also hear that wondrous faith in human creativity. In these abstractions lies a sensitivity to concreteness that could only be achieved by a poet capable of thinking of the work of another. In the depths of Senghor's feelings for the works of Soulages is that mysterious admiration and awe which a thinker or artist receives from the creative powers of a fellow creator. If we don't begin with given theological dispositions, then our sensitivity to man's creative powers are derived wholly from the works and activities themselves. In speaking of Soulages, Senghor noted some questions which applied to Soulages's work. "We would ask," Senghor said, "if he began with nature and abstracted from it its qualities, or if he created a world, we dare say, gratuitously. We would even ask if he expressed ideas, sentiments, or simple sensations. We would finally ask if he were an architect, musician, or painter." In reply to these questions, Senghor said: "*Pierre*

[11]"La Puissance créatrice de Pierre Soulages," in *Liberté* 3:553.

Soulages is a pure painter, that is, a poet." We explain his art by speaking of "his poetic genius: his creative power."[12]

We would imagine that it is in these creative powers that we discover our closeness to the divine, but we could also say that it is in them that we find the marvels of man. Yet we know there are limits, there is despair and renunciation. Human powers fade. They fail to find the appreciation and love which nurture and give them life. In the moments of glory lie pain and disappointment. The glory of man remains ephemeral. It comes to us fleetingly and passes from us quickly. Man has always known how passing is every human possession. He has heard this from the ancient wisdom that hovers over life but is rarely heeded by those who hear it. We hear sounds but not words. From Koheleth, the son of David, the hearer of sayings, we listen to these words: "A Wise Man, however, will bear in mind that there is a time of doom. For there is a time for every experience, including the doom; for a man's calamity overwhelms him. Indeed, he does not know what is to happen, even where it is on the point of happening, who can tell him? No man has authority over his life breath – to hold back the life breath, there is no authority over the day of death. There is no mustering out from that war; wealth is powerless to save its owner" (Eccles. 8:6-9).

A sensitivity to man's finiteness is the foundation for a sensitive appreciation of his achievements. In man there is a persistent sense of uncertainty that permeates life from day to day. When we write and describe the realities man has accomplished, we do it with admiration and expectation for their continuity. We know that men have sought to explain the nature of their existence, the meaning of the earth and heaven which encompasses them, through myths. They have sought to create an autonomous realm in which man discovers that within the self there are sufficient powers to explore the world and give it meaning. There is a decisive text of Senghor entitled "The Aesthetic of the Negro-African" (1956) which reveals how profoundly perceptive he was to these elements in African life, and it was from this perceptiveness that there emerged his realization that a world order was possible only if we understood intelligently, if we could become aware of, the cultural contributions of various peoples. Senghor stated: "We are always concerned with a relationship, either with totemistic ancestor or with mythic spirits. But the spirit often has the characteristics of the star and the animal, and the legend is deepened in the myth." Senghor spoke of the importance of initiation into "the cosmological myths, the legends and the customs of the tribe." "Then," he said, "the seed dies to be reborn, the child dies unto itself to be reborn the adult in the initiator of

[12]Ibid., 557.

the ancestor. We are dealing with a *religious, animalistic existentialism.* The Other, the adult, the Ancestor, the spirit or God, far from being the obstacle is the support, the source of vital force. Far from there being a confrontation between I and Thou, there is a reconciling accord. Rather than a nonrealization, there is the greatest realization of the human essence."[13]

The beliefs that Senghor described are a microcosm of ours. They bear the totems, the myths, the legends, and the ancestors that animate present society. But, above all, they reveal the primeval pantheism which has always answered man's need for an intimate and present God. Although we have seen this presence take on many forms and shades, we know that the foods from the heavens find their way to earth, and become the nourishment of our existence. But materialism has often drawn us away from the totems which belonged to the gods. It gives us the illusion of the divine man who has finally conquered the gods of the nether world and returned man to his sovereignty. Man's punishment is over, the mark of Cain is erased.

The force of Maritain's analysis lies in his challenge to man's longing for self-deification. In particular, it is the poet and the writer who more often than not seek this exaggerated self-glorification. "With Mallarmé and Valéry," Maritain noted, "the options for the rejection of transcendence taught modern poetry the experience of the void (and also, as concerns Mallarmé, a faint hope in magic). I wonder whether the Olympus of words to whose mysterious rites the great mind of Joyce dedicated itself, did not emerge from some similar experience of the void – and a haunting memory of a lost paradise guarded by the sword of a fiery Irish angel."[14]

The story of man's struggle with God is ancient. It goes back to Jacob and we hear Jacob's words: "I will not let you go unless you bless me," and Jacob was given the name Israel "for you have striven with beings divine and human" (Gen. 32:27). Here lies the destiny of man, the forceful striving with God through which man discovers himself and his eternal destiny. The striving is not only with the self, but with God at a *place* called Peniel, meaning "I have seen a divine being face to face yet my life has been spared." The world of biblical imagery and faith creates its own milieu. Maritain's challenge to the poets, to Rimbaud, Baudelaire, Valéry, Mallarmé, is to men for whom the biblical world was never alive. It had no place in them. Its blood never flowed through their being, and the texts never became part of their spirit. These men belonged to a secular world, dominated by the powers of reason, and it was to that

---

[13]"The Aesthetic of the Negro-African," *Liberté* 1:206.
[14]*Creative Intuition in Art and Poetry*, 179.

world they gave their love. The poet, like every other being, has his place of initiation, his totems and tabus, and from them he fills and nourishes his life.

We listen to the Psalmists, we read their poems, and we find that these poets have no need of new myths. They believe the old beliefs are still meaningful. These poets emerge from a faith in the creation and in the God who is present in history, who judges and influences the lives of men, and the course of the universe. The Psalmists come into a world that is comprehensible, where chaos becomes order. Man understands that his reason is his most precious gift, and his moral responsibilities are its expression. Man knows that this obligation is in all men, and in this universal obligation man finds the natural law that unites humankind into a family and a community. The poet is not the seeker of a new mythology in which he discovers himself and his place in the universe. He is the poet who sings of the eternal order, who is forced to find the meaning of creation, knowing that his God is always present. The poet adores the power of the word as a gift of God. He sees that his talent lies in the service of the divine. He struggles with the divine like Jacob forcing from God a blessing, the power to do even more beautifully the work of man. The poet knows a profound truth. The Psalmist enunciated it: "O Lord, You have been our refuge in every generation. Before the mountains came into being, before You brought forth the earth and the world from eternity to eternity You are God" (Ps. 90). Alive in these words is a poetic reverie that accompanies us from work to work and from belief to belief. From this anchorage, we construct the world and find its beauty.

Nothing brought Senghor closer to Maritain than the rejection of materialism. The poet found in the philosopher's thought an attempt to discover the interrelationship between man and God, between nature and grace. A separation made by the intellect and its natural skepticism was not acceptable to the poet who from his African tradition had always known how intimate and conscious was the divine presence in nature. What the intellect separates and analyzes, the feelings bring together and hold in union. The world is animated by powers that lie beyond the realm of man's creative forces. Man's creative forces are forces that come from the heavens and fructify man and the earth. Not only do we raise our hands toward the sky, but the sky comes toward us and nourishes the longing which moves our feelings upwards. But divine forces live not only above us, but surround us. They permeate what we see and hear, what we smell and taste. There is a transubstantiation which we find in faith and in our arts: the song, the dance, the poem, the initiation, and the rites. Man is capable of approaching the divine on many levels, and it is through his senses that he feels the divine presence that dwells among and in created things.

Senghor's Catholic Christianity modifies the pantheism that is so precious to those who have not lost the intimacy between God and man. Christianity reopens the realm of the intellect and attempts to bring it into harmony, but not into identification, with faith. Maritain was dedicated to reason and grace, to the divine and the human, to creation and the creator. Senghor was introduced to a philosophy which found a place for every human activity, which comprehended the power of grace, as well as of reason, which spoke of divine, natural, and positive law, which embodied political as well as moral and social responsibility. The grandeur of St. Thomas made it possible for every man to find a place and a meaning within the architecture. Only those who sought to radicalize oppositions, to exaggerate the powers of reason or faith, would find it difficult to dwell with St. Thomas. This was not a "set table but a philosophy in motion." Each thinker would find a new way to express his devotion to St. Thomas.

From this philosophy, Maritain elucidated his own thinking. He clarified with care the difference between poetry and metaphysics. This he did in *The Frontiers of Poetry,* and these distinctions would remain the landmarks of his thought. Although Senghor refers only to his *Integral Humanism,* it is in *The Frontiers of Poetry* that the core of Maritain's aesthetics is enunciated. Maritain stated: "This divination of the spiritual in the things of the senses, and which expresses itself in the things of the senses, is precisely what we call *poetry.* Metaphysics too pursues a spiritual prey, but in a very different manner, and with a very different formal object. Whereas metaphysics stands in the line of *knowledge* and of the contemplation of truth, poetry stands in the line of *making* and of the delight procured by beauty."[15]

Whether this destination is valid demands a theoretical discussion which would be settled through the spiritual weight of either the poet or the metaphysician. What is important is that both elements of human activity reveal to us something that is fundamental about man, the thinker and the maker. Poetry is making. It is formed by the precious sounds which man molds with his words. Here the utilitarian quality of prose is subordinated to the rhythm and preciosity of the imagery which words evoke, or the emotive forces from which they are born. Poetry touches that demon within us. In the word he is revealed. It is formed by that phoenixlike quality which is eternal life through death, birth through rebirth. If poetry is separated from the form of knowledge that is sought in metaphysics, it is because the poetic is eternal in its process

[15]*The Frontiers of Poetry,* 128.

and not through pure universality. What we seek in metaphysics we would transfigure in poetry. Through the latter we are brought close to the senses, to a world bubbling with imagery. Knowledge is a purification from the world of feeling and emotion; it aims at the purest of all ideas: I am what I am, I am truth. Poetry is born again in every spirit because it has died in it. Knowledge is learned with rigor and intensity and remains in its fixity. What we cultivate in poetry is sensitivity and imagination, what we cultivate in knowledge is abstraction and differentiation. But these two directions of the spirit are in man irreconcilable ways of comprehension. They lead to no harmony, but only to a disharmony. In this disharmony man is truly the maker, the creator of an architecture in which the forms harmonize only through contrasts. In other words, through their oppositions, they show the nature of their dependence and belonging.

Maritain regarded the difference between poetry and metaphysics seriously. "Metaphysics," he said, "snatches at the spiritual in an idea, by the most abstract intellection; poetry reaches it in the flesh, by the very point of the sense sharpened through intelligence. Metaphysics enjoys its possession only in the retreats of the eternal regions, while poetry finds its own at every crossroad in the wanderings of the contingent and the singular.... Metaphysics gives chase to essences and definitions, poetry to any flash of existence glittering by the way, and any reflection of an invisible order. Metaphysics isolates mystery in order to know it; poetry, thanks to the balances it constructs, handles and utilizes mystery as an unknown force."[16]

While metaphysics chases the definition, the a priori statement, the principle, poetry seeks the world of the senses to find the hidden divine sparks. In this it is like St. Francis, who was "so overflowing with charity that he loved not only his fellowmen, but all fellow creatures – birds, beasts, fishes and even creeping things – for in each one of them he perceived the handiwork of his Father, and if he chanced to see anything suffering pain, he too, suffered with it."[17] This love of what has been called "the contingent and the singular" is the poetry of creation. Distinct and different from the world of the intellect and its careful precise clarity, the poetical is in love with the particular in its joyful and painful existence, in what can be felt, heard, and seen. It lives from the specific, from the lost and desperate which is in search of companionship and harmony, of love and tenderness. The intellect is the marvel of brightness and perfection. It has no tenderness nor compassion. It has surpassed the

---

[16]Ibid.

[17]*The Wisdom of St. Frances and His Companions* (New York: A New Directions Book, 1978), 41.

individual and dwells only in the universal from which it surveys with majestic splendor the insignificant ways of the lost and wandering creature. The contrast is profound between the poetical and the metaphysical, between the longing of the intellect for purity, that is, the absence of doubt, and the poetical love of the existent with all its subtle possibilities and forms. "Above all inanimate creatures, Francis loved the sun and fire with most devotion, for he used to say: In the morning when the sun rises everyone ought to praise God who created him for our good, for him our eyes are enlightened by day; and in the evening when night comes on, everyone ought to give praise for Brother Fire, because by him our eyes are enlightened at night."[18]

In these marvels of the universe, what we see becomes the inspiration of imagery. Men have always contemplated the sun and fire, and in meditation upon them, the divine and the human have always found dwellings with each other. Senghor knew how deeply tied the spirit was to the physical, how the poet sought a way from one to the other, and how deeply he needed the marvel of the word to bring them into harmony. The intellect needs always to be brought back from the search for the sun. Its wings are waxen and they disappear quickly as the intellect is enticed to move closer and closer to the unseeable truth that can be looked upon only by divine beings. The intellect has to be held back from the forbidden tree. But the physical has also a corruptive power that grows as we became more and more immersed in it. Our eyes and ears lose their vision and can no longer look up and meditate upon the heavens. In defiance of their limits the physical becomes demonic.

Maritain's reflections come in the form of warnings. He reminds the artist and the poet that they are not divine creators, but only translators of reality. The beauty that they bring forth lies in the creation. The artist and the poet are divine helpers in whose works the creation yields marvels that are both beyond and coextensive with nature. The creation yields to reformation and transformation. It is the source of unending change and beauty. Man, the artist, finds within himself both the poet and the metaphysician. With these spiritual powers, he reveals the depths of the divine seeds that lie scattered through nature.

We cannot point to a specific element of Maritain's thought and say: Here is the point of Senghor's inspiration. Senghor referred specifically to Maritain's book *Integral Humanism: Temporal and Spiritual Problems of a New Humanism* because the direction of Senghor's thought was toward the formation of the idea of humanism. Like a watchman of the human flock, Senghor realized that between the ideal and the real there was a heroic dialogue. The more the real with its concern for material

---

[18]Ibid., 65-66.

satisfaction, with its involvement in political and social realities, required decision and courage, absorbing within itself the totality of human existence, the more the poet, the thinker, realized that the real lies in the faith of the ideal. The latter demanded a strength of commitment rarely achieved among men, a tolerance of spiritual isolation that was often difficult to bear. Yet the voice of faith remains constant and persistent. It grows in assurance as the opposition increases. Even in surrender it knows a justification of the struggle, but also the weakness of existence.

Senghor became the lonely prophet in a world of political and moral intrigue. His voice remains stronger than ever and if there is an answer to Maritain's question: "Is a heroic human possible?" it can only be in the affirmative. Spiritual life is not quietude, a withdrawal from reality. Socrates could not be tempted to leave the scene of his spiritual life. Crito pleaded with him, but he refused. Senghor never leaves his fellowmen without the presence of his word, without the feeling that he is ever-present where the struggle for universality has to be fought. Maritain noted in reference to the struggle which always must be fought: "And I wonder if it is not in the answer to this question (and the ground one gives for it) that depends above all on the different positions taken by various men in the face of the historical work which is taking place before our eyes, and the diverse practical options to which they feel themselves obliged."[19]

The humanism which Maritain embraced was rooted in the dignity of the person. This dignity is derived not simply from the individual, but from the divine image that dwells within him. Driven either by a demon or by the belief in God's presence, man views his place in the universe as the consequence of a divine human destiny. This destiny emerges from ties that link us to our ancestors and the continuity of faith. No escape from this responsibility is possible without the infliction of grave harm upon the spirit. Where the spirit causes us to reject the values of the temporal order, there the spirit is wounded and diminished. We remember how Abraham stood before the cities of Sodom and Gomorrah and pleaded with God to protect them from destruction if even five righteous men could be found. Spiritual and temporal life belong to each other. In exaggerated worship of either the state or the spiritual life, the individual is distorted. A gross evil fills the world. Maritain noted that "it is not to the dynamism or the imperialism of race or class or nation that this humanism asks men to sacrifice themselves; it is to a better life for their brothers and to the concrete good of the community of human persons; it is to the humble truth of brotherly love to be realized – all at

---

[19]*Integral Humanism*, trans. Joseph W. Evans (New York: Charles Scribner's, 1968), 4.

the cost of an always difficult effort and of a relative poverty – in the social order and the structures of common life. In this way such a humanism can make man grow in communion, and if so, it cannot be less than a heroic humanism."[20]

Humanism is inseparable from the loneliness and heroism of the righteous. For in the midst of the entire community of men it is the righteous that remain the source of salvation. The divine will quietly endure in those who live without righteousness for it will also be their redemption. Abraham reveals to us the source of heroic humanism, he shows us how the few become the force and inspiration for the many, how righteousness is more than blind justice, how it discovers the person in the individual, the community in the group. It is a simple trust in the divine Word to refuse to harm your fellowman. It reveals the humanity which every man should embody, if only inadequately and partially. Every person is responsible for the humanity he bears within. In 1943, Maritain again elaborated upon this heroic humanism. He reminded us that "it is up to the supreme effort of human freedom in the mortal struggle in which it is today engaged, to see to it that the age which we are entering is not the age of the masses and of the shapeless multitudes nourished and brought into subjection and led to the slaughter by infamous demigods, but rather the age of the people and the man of common humanity, cognizant of the dignity of the human person in himself, builder of a more human world directed toward an historic ideal of human brotherhood."[21]

If we think of Senghor, his imagery, and his idealism, we cannot but believe that his life has been filled with not only a heroic but a humane humanism. We imagine Abraham standing before God pleading for the world, asking that righteousness redeem its powers of progress and innovation. We see him wink at Senghor with a smile, and say to him in silent, but potent, words: You are a righteous man. You live humanely. For the sake of people such as you, the world will go on and humankind will have a renewed chance to draw from itself the hope and trust and, above all, the action which are in the righteous. The creation rediscovers its divine force and evolution, and the divine presence is again the light to the human soul in the ways of those whose actions have refused to betray their fellow beings through either indifference or cowardice.

Man has always sung of this light. In his *Book of Life*, Marsilio Ficino, who loved Plato dearly, remarked: "As our dear Plato says, no sight is ever visible at all unless something on high is visible in it, that is, some

---

[20]Ibid., 7.

[21]*Christianity and Democracy* and *The Rights of Man and Natural Law* (San Francisco: Ignatius Press, 1986), 83-4.

splendor of the sun itself. The human intellect never apprehends anything intelligible unless there is something intelligible in it from on high, the light of God always and forever present for us. A light, I say, which illumines every man who comes into the world. A light which David sings of: In your light we shall see light."[22]

---

[22]*The Book of Life* (Dallas: Spring Publications, 1988), 35.

Conclusion

Every great literary work is a conversation not only with another, with a past or the self, but it is a memory in which the *I* searches to discover the meaning of the conversation. A book comes from the desire both to speak and to listen. Silence gives us the solitude we deeply need to dream of our conversations, to dream of the images they bring forth and will continue to create. We are men through the Word and the Word has been through the ages both body and soul. Again and again we hear the words of the Gospelist: *Et Verbum caro factum est, et habitavit in nobis* (all that came to be was alive with his life, and that life was the light of men). The Word dwells among us, and to our colleague and companion we ask about the word that is enunciated and which is given us as our possession. With Senghor, we have read the many words embodied in poems, essays, books, interviews, and speeches. We are asked to give our impressions of them, explain to others what they mean, and we are pained and distraught because these words have meant so many different things to us at each stage of our writing and thinking. We find that we must settle for a few formulas which indicate to the readers where, at the moment, we place the greater stress. I would imagine that if we turned to Senghor's concise book *Ce que je crois,* we would find those hooks upon which we can hang some thoughts, and could give a few signs to those who want to know where we have journeyed with Senghor. With this in mind, I would conclude with a quotation from this book and offer a brief commentary.

Senghor speaks often of African thought as a humanism. This word embraces a prophet's vision of a renewed humankind, and it is from this vision that Senghor tells us the message he has for his fellowman, which must be carried through the continents, to those who wait to hear the words that will bring enlightenment to the soul. Speaking of African philosophy, Senghor reminds us that "man is the active center of the cosmos. His essential human function is to capture all the scattered forces which lie at the ground of matter, all the aspects, the forms and colors, odors and movements, sounds, noises, tremblings, and silences of the universe. He must reinforce their life by enhancing their force. The undefinable word Life, in essence, explains African philosophy, its art and religion. Man helps God's force and becomes similar to Him. He animates, through art, the visible and invisible universe, singing about it, giving it rhythms. It is for this reason that the Africans say, 'God needs man,' that is, he needs men and humankind."[1]

Senghor speaks the memories of the African man. His books are written before he writes them. History has already left him its accounts. He struggles to give them form, to allow the French language to make these accounts communicable to humankind. Senghor found his companions among the great figures of French literature; in the philosophers, the poets, the painters, and above all, in the startling figure of Teilhard de Chardin. France was not a limit, he wandered in the lands of the English, the Spanish. Neither Asia nor the Middle East were beyond his purview. He was present wherever man formed cultures, and his presence caused him to see and hear how the inflow and outflow of cultures create the civilization of the universal. We have little to conclude, but much to awaken. There is much that needs to be said about humankind, so much that belongs to us physically and spiritually, and so much which we need to acquire. We cannot allow ourselves to be trapped by preformed fixities. We learn from Senghor, as we learn from our ongoing conversations that we are always at a distance from what we are going to say; we need to catch up and find a relationship between what we have said and the reality we believe we have spoken about. In some way, there is always a gap, an unbridgeable one, that never seems to be filled in. This is not our despair; it is our journey to the reality of our being. Senghor knows how to read his companions. He fought with them for a prize, and like Jacob he received one. He gained the power to write well.

What fascinates the reader about Senghor is the realization that what he is being told seems to have already been revealed to the poet. Senghor speaks the poetic-religious traditions of the African, but with it he tells the story of another great literature. He, like a master juggler, balances the two, not wanting one to yield to the other. Between them stands the poet, the master player who knows that both are necessary for his survival. The story of the juggling is the marvel and mystery of this great poet-politician. Few of us would want to imitate him, few of us could. We are sensitive to the voices which come from many lands and find a dwelling within him. We observe how he listens to the past, how his listening guides his pen, and how writing and hearing become one.

---

[1]*Ce que je crois*, 113.

Senghor shows us how to read by showing us the art of writing, the drawing together of rhythm, sounds and images, song and dance, life and thought.

I believe that every true reader is a writer. I believe that Senghor is a poet and writer with whom we read and write like companions in search of truth. We discover that truth is always beyond us, and what we have are signs and symbols. We travel with the poet, leaving behind the signs so that others can follow. We are pleased with our journeys because the poet fascinates us with the beauty of his words and the magnificence of his visions. He teaches us how to listen and to see. We ask no more of him.